Tell Me about the Catholic Faith

From the Bible to the Sacraments

Ignatius • MAGNIFICAT®

Under the direction of
Most Reverend Michel Dubost
Christine Pedotti and Romain Lizé

Contributing Authors:
Jean Mercier
Caroline Paschal
Bruno Le Sourd
Diane de Vinols
Karine-Marie Voyer
Virginie Wicker

Translation by:
Janet Chevrier

Editors:
Vivian Dudro
Isabelle Galmiche

Layout Design:
Céline Ambroselli

Layout:
Elise Borel

Production:
Sabine Marioni

This book is for you.

I hope that you are curious and want to grow! The people who wrote this book are grown-ups: some are old enough to be your big brother, or your parent. And I am probably almost old enough to be your grandfather.

But it is in friendship that we have written this book. We are all of us living a wonderful adventure. And we aren't the only ones, nor the first ones!

This is why we wished to share these stories—so you can join in this adventure too!

Our adventure has a name: Jesus.

For us, he is the way, the truth, and the life.

Even if we are already grown up, he makes us grow even more!

Even if we know lots of things, he makes us curious to know more.

Have a wonderful journey!

Most Reverend Michel Dubost

Contents

1. The Bible
The Great Book of Christians

2. The Christian Faithful
The History of the Church

3. The Catholic Faith
The Beliefs and Sacraments

1

The Bible

The Great Book of Christians

The Bible
A True Story of Love

The Bible is a large work. An entire library of seventy-three books is contained within its covers! Each of them tells part of the true story of a great mystery: how God came to befriend all men and women.

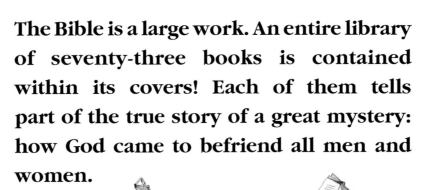

The adventures of God's friends

In the Bible, we read about the breathtaking adventures of God's friends. There is Noah, who saved his family from the flood, and Abraham, who was prepared to give up his own son but became the father of God's people. Moses freed God's people from slavery, and young David fought the giant Goliath and was chosen to be king. Prophets such as Elijah spoke in the name of God and worked wonders, while others foretold the coming of the Savior. Finally, Jesus, the Son of God, came into the world to save mankind.

The Word of God

The first stories in the Bible are very old. At first, they were passed down through many generations, from parents to their children. Later, when God

gave Moses the Ten Commandments, these stories were written in what is called the Old Testament. Much later, the first Christians wrote down the story of Jesus and the Church; this is the New Testament. The Gospels tell how Jesus lived and died and rose from the dead. The books that follow the Gospels show us how the friends of Jesus proclaimed this good news to the whole world!

The Spirit of God inspired those who wrote the Bible so that everyone could know the story of God's friendship with mankind. Thus, the Bible is the Word of God. The same Holy Spirit helps the Church to believe and to teach what God says to us through the Bible. When we hear and read the Bible, the Holy Spirit speaks to our hearts and draws us near to God.

Writing!

A long time ago, people did not write on paper. People living on the banks of the Euphrates River in Mesopotamia made tablets out of clay on which they inscribed text using a stylus. Near the Nile River in Egypt, people formed the river reed papyrus into paper-like sheets upon which they could write. Later, people made parchment out of sheep or goat skin: they removed the fur and tanned the skin to make a smooth writing surface. In the time of Jesus, the Old Testament was written on long parchment scrolls, which could be unrolled as they were read.

God Created the World
Six Very Busy Days

The first pages of the Bible tell how God created everything. The story of Creation is in the book of Genesis. The word *genesis* means "beginning".

In the beginning, God created heaven and earth. The earth was dark and empty, and the Spirit of God swept over the surface of the water. Then God said, "Let there be light!" And light burst forth. There was evening and then morning—it was the first day.

God said, "Let there be sky!" And so it happened. Evening came, and then morning—it was the second day.

God said, "Let there be the earth, and let there be the seas!" Then he said, "Let the earth put forth grass and all kinds of plants and trees!" And so it happened. And God saw that is was good. Evening came, and then morning—it was the third day.

God said, "Let there be a sun for the day, and a moon and stars for the night!" God made the sun, the moon, and the stars. He saw that it was good. And there was evening, and then there was morning—it was the fourth day.

God said, "Let creatures fill the waters, and let birds fly through the sky!" And God created all the creatures that live in the waters and all those that fly in the sky. He saw that it was good. There was evening, and then morning—it was the fifth day.

God said, "Let the earth be full of animals, from snakes that crawl to four-legged beasts!" God made all the animals that live on the earth, and he saw that it was good.

Then God said, "Let us make man in our image, after our own likeness." And so he created man, both male and female. He blessed the first man and woman and said to them, "Have many children! I place in your care the fish of the sea, the birds of the sky, and all living creatures that move upon the earth! I give you the plants and the trees for your food." And so it was. And God saw that everything was very good! Then evening came, and then morning—it was the sixth day.

And on the seventh day, God rested from all the work he had done.

What is the truth?

Today, experts say that the world was not created in six days but evolved over billions of years. It is good that scientists try to explain these things, because the Bible is meant to explain something much more important: God wants there to be an earth, animals, and above all, men and women. It matters little how long creation took; the most important truth is that God loves all that he has made.

The Flood
Noah and the Ark

One day, the first man and woman— Adam and Eve—chose to disobey God. This first sin hurt man's friendship with God. Jealousy, hatred, and fighting spread everywhere. God finally had enough and decided to remake the world with the help of Noah.

God chose Noah

Noah was a good and righteous man. One morning, God said to him, "Build a big boat, an ark made of wood, with a door to enter through and a roof to cover it. When it is ready, take a pair of every sort of animal and bird, a male and a female, and put them into the ark. Then you too board the ark with your wife, your three sons, and their wives—and take plenty of food for yourselves and the animals."

Forty days and forty nights

Noah obeyed and did as God commanded. When everyone had boarded the ark, the rains began to fall from the skies. There was such a storm that it lasted forty days and forty nights! It was a flood. Noah's ark floated on the waters, and soon the whole surface of the earth was covered. All the animals and people that were not in the ark were drowned.

God blessed Noah

At last one day, the rain stopped falling. Little by little, the water subsided, and the ark came to rest on top of a mountain. Noah sent out a dove to see how far the waters had gone down. It came back with a fresh olive branch in its beak—that was a good sign! Noah waited another seven days and sent the dove out again; it did not return. With that, Noah knew for sure: the whole earth must be dry again. God said to Noah, "Leave the ark with your family and the animals." Then God blessed him, saying, "Now, may your children have many children! And may all the animals breed abundantly! May the earth be filled again!"

The rainbow

God promised Noah: "I will never again send a flood to destroy mankind. Instead, I make between us a pact of love, a covenant. I will set a rainbow in the clouds as a sign of this covenant."

Abraham
Father of God's People

Abraham was an old man. Sarah, his wife, was old too and had not given birth to any children. They lived among their tribe near the banks of the Euphrates River. One day, God called Abraham.

God's promise

God said to Abraham, "Go to the land that I will show to you. I will make a nation of you, and, thanks to you, all the families of the earth shall be blessed." Abraham believed what God had told him and left with his wife and some relatives. When Abraham arrived in Canaan, God made a covenant with him: "Look at the land around you. I give it to you and to your children and to your children's children. They will be my people." Abraham was astonished and said, "But Lord, I don't have any children!" Then God promised, "Your children will be as numerous as the grains of sand on the seashore and the stars in the sky."

Sarah's laughter

One day, Abraham saw three men nearing his camp. He ran to them, bowed at their feet, and said, "Stay, wash your feet, rest yourselves, and have something to eat. Quick, Sarah, bake them some bread!" Then he prepared a roast calf for his guests. When the

Abraham, father of all who believe in God

God told Abraham that he would have many children. The story of Abraham is known by billions of believers throughout the world. Jews, Christians, and Muslims all call themselves children of Abraham.

meal was over, one of the visitors said, "In a year's time, your wife will have a son." Inside the tent, Sarah laughed to herself: "Me! I'm too old to have a child!" Then the visitor added, "Why did Sarah laugh? Nothing is impossible for God!" Some months later, Sarah gave birth to a son. Abraham named him Isaac, which means "the one who laughs", because of Sarah's laughter.

A test of faith

Isaac grew up. One day, God called to Abraham, "Take your only son and go to the mountain. I want you to sacrifice him to me." Abraham saddled his donkey and left. On the mountaintop, he tied Isaac to a woodpile and raised his knife. Then a voice broke from the skies: "Don't do anything to the boy! Now I know that you refuse God nothing." Abraham spotted a ram caught by its horns in the bushes, and he sacrificed it in place of Isaac.

Later, Isaac married the beautiful Rebekah. The covenant with God continued through them and their son Jacob, who was later called Israel.

Is God cruel?

We remember the story of Abraham and Isaac to remind ourselves that God does not want human sacrifices. He does not want parents to kill their children. Rather, he wants men and women to trust him to the end, even when a situation seems impossible.

Moses
Son of a Hebrew Slave

The descendants of Abraham, Isaac, and Jacob—the Hebrews—fled to a foreign land to escape a famine in their country. They settled in Egypt on the banks of the Nile. After many years of happiness, disaster struck: Pharaoh, the king of Egypt, enslaved them!

A baby in a basket

"There are too many of these Hebrews!" Pharaoh declared to his officers. "Someday they could make war on us. Let us make them our slaves." But the Hebrews continued to multiply. So Pharaoh ordered that all the newborn Hebrew boys be thrown into the Nile.

One Hebrew mother hid her infant son for three months. When she could hide him no longer, she wove a watertight basket. She laid the baby in it, placed it on the river, and had her daughter watch over it nearby.

A short time later, Pharaoh's daughter came to bathe in the river. She uncovered the basket and understood: "It's a Hebrew baby boy! I must save him!" The baby's sister came forward and said, "Would you like me to find someone to nurse him?" The princess agreed and, without knowing it, entrusted the baby back to his mother.

The princess named the baby Moses, which means "saved from the waters", and she loved him like a son.

Many years later, Moses saw an Egyptian beating a Hebrew slave. In a fit of rage, he killed the Egyptian. By the next day, the whole town had heard about it. Fearing the anger of Pharaoh, Moses ran far away into the desert.

A burning bush

Moses became a shepherd in the land of Midian. One day, as he was leading his flock through the mountains, he saw an amazing sight: a fire in the middle of a bush, but the bush did not burn up! Moses went to look at it, and the voice of God spoke from the bush: "Moses, I have heard the cry of my people! I am going to deliver them from their sufferings! I will bring them out of Egypt! They will enter a beautiful and fruitful land. Now, go see Pharaoh and tell him that the Lord says, 'Let my people go.' " Moses was terrified, but God reassured him, "I will be with you. You will say to the Hebrews that I am the God of Abraham, Isaac, and Jacob. And this is my name: 'I AM WHO I AM.' " Moses took these mysterious words to heart, and without delay he set off to Egypt to fulfill his mission.

Egypt of the pharaohs

Ancient Egypt was a vast country whose many inhabitants lived crowded together along the banks of the Nile, for the rest of the land was nothing but desert. Egypt was a rich warrior nation. The kings, called pharaohs, had such power that they seemed like gods. The pharaoh in the story of Moses is thought to have been Ramses II.

Moses
The Journey to Freedom

Moses had to convince the king of Egypt to let the Hebrews go, but Pharaoh was a hard-hearted man.

Pharaoh was very stubborn

Moses could plead all he wanted; Pharaoh would not listen! "You are my slaves. What do I care about your God?" So Moses worked wonders to convince Pharaoh. One morning, he turned his rod into a snake just by throwing it on the ground. Pharaoh only sneered! Then Moses struck the Nile, and the water turned into blood. Next came thousands of frogs, gnats, and flies. The livestock died, and the people broke out in boils. Thunder, hail, and fire rained upon the earth, and then locusts followed by darkness covered the land. Still Pharaoh refused to obey God.

The Passover

Then God told the Hebrews to eat quickly some roasted lamb and unleavened bread. It was the Passover, when death would pass over their homes while striking those of the Egyptians. That night the firstborn of each Egyptian family died, and at last Pharaoh let the Hebrews go. With Moses leading the way, they marched through the desert until they reached the Red Sea. Pharaoh changed his mind and chased after them with his army, but before he could reach them, God stirred up a great wind that split

the waters of the sea in two. The Hebrews crossed on dry land, but the waters closed over Pharaoh and his army, and they were drowned. God's people were finally free!

Manna in the desert

The march through the desert was long, and the Hebrews grew weary. "We're thirsty! We're hungry!" they cried. Moses struck a rock with his rod, and water gushed out. God sent little birds—quails—for the people to eat and also a bread-like food called manna. Each day, the people ate their fill.

God forgave his people

God called Moses up a mountain and gave him the Ten Commandments, engraved on two stone tablets. When Moses went back down to his people, he found them worshipping a golden calf as though it were a god! In anger, Moses smashed the tablets. Fortunately, God was forgiving. He gave Moses the Ten Commandments again, as well as many other laws. He also renewed his covenant with his people, who placed the new tablets in a precious box: the Ark of the Covenant.

After a forty-year march through the desert, the Hebrews arrived within sight of the Promised Land, the same country God had given to Abraham and his descendants.

The Ten Commandments

1. You shall have no other gods besides me. You shall not make images of other gods and worship them.
2. You shall not take the name of the Lord in vain.
3. Remember the Sabbath day, and keep it holy.
4. Honor your father and your mother.
5. You shall not kill.
6. You shall not commit adultery.
7. You shall not steal.
8. You shall not accuse another falsely.
9. You shall not covet your neighbor's husband or wife.
10. You shall not covet your neighbor's goods.

The Promised Land
A Garden in the Desert

Before dying, Moses beheld the wonderful land God had promised.

The land of Canaan, also called the land of Israel, is nestled like a little garden between the Mediterranean Sea and the desert to the east. The long Jordan River flows through the country, watering the oases. Everything grows there: palm, fig, orange, and lemon trees with their delicious fruits to eat. In the distance, the pink and golden mountains of the land of Judea bloom with flowers in the spring. The Dead Sea is a surprising place: its water is so salty that nothing can live in it, and when you swim in it, you float!

The hillsides of the land of Canaan were planted with grapevines and olive trees. From the grapevines came wine to cheer the heart. From the olive trees, with their wrinkly trunks and silvery leaves, came a fruit that could be

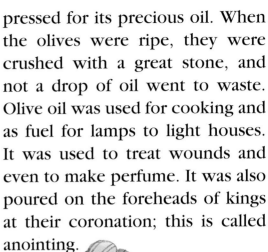

pressed for its precious oil. When the olives were ripe, they were crushed with a great stone, and not a drop of oil went to waste. Olive oil was used for cooking and as fuel for lamps to light houses. It was used to treat wounds and even to make perfume. It was also poured on the foreheads of kings at their coronation; this is called anointing.

Camels crossed the desert carrying their precious cargo to faraway lands. Treasures such as cinnamon and salt, silk fabrics and jewels, beans and wheat, pistachios and almonds were all transported in earthenware jars or in leather chests. At the wells, travelers would stop to drink and rest themselves; shepherds led their flocks of sheep and goats there, and families pitched tents nearby. The well was also a meeting place for boys and girls who would sometimes fall in love and get married.

David
The Greatest King of Israel

Three thousand years ago, David became king of Israel. He founded a great, rich, and powerful kingdom. He chose Jerusalem, the most beautiful city in the land, to be its capital. And yet David was just a shepherd boy when it all began.

The boy who would be king

One day, I was keeping the sheep out in the fields when one of my father's servants arrived out of breath. "Quick, your father is waiting for you. The old prophet Samuel is looking for a new king of Israel, and he wants to see you." My father presented me to Samuel, and my seven older brothers laughed, "Have you ever seen such a little king?" Samuel looked at me and said, "I anoint your head with this oil; you will be king. God has chosen you."

David and Bathsheba

A musician and a warrior, David was good at everything. But David was not perfect. Listen to his story.

David was very brave

The giant Goliath terrified the soldiers of Israel, but David was not afraid. He knew that God was with him. Using his slingshot, David hurled a rock at Goliath's forehead, and the giant fell to the ground. Then David cut off Goliath's head.

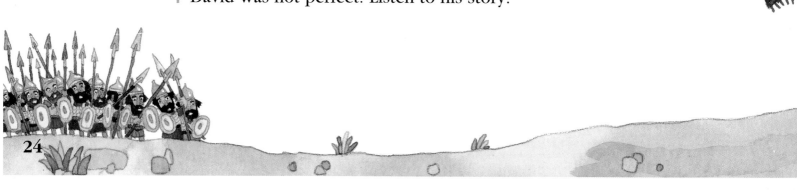

One evening, from the roof of my palace, I saw a very beautiful woman bathing. She was as lovely as a queen, and I fell madly in love with her. I found out that she was Bathsheba, the wife of Uriah, the captain of my guards. That made no difference to me. I wanted to marry her, and nothing and no one could stop me, not even the laws of God that I knew and loved in my heart. Bathsheba became my wife, and I sent Uriah off to be killed in the war. The prophet Nathan came to me and asked, "What would you think of a very rich man who stole from a poor man his most precious possession—his little lamb?" I said he would deserve to die. Then Nathan said, "That man is you. You stole from Uriah his wife and his life!" Suddenly, I understood the terrible wrongs that I had done. I was so ashamed; I wished the earth would swallow me up. I wept, and I prayed to God for forgiveness.

David loved God

David never forgot the Lord. He composed very beautiful prayers, called psalms, which are like conversations with God. He dreamed of building a house for the worship of God in Jerusalem. In the end, it was his son Solomon who oversaw its construction. The Temple took seven years and a great many workers to build.

25

Psalms
Speaking to God as Lord and Friend

The book of Psalms is a collection of heartfelt conversations with God. There are psalms to tell God everything we experience: trust, anger, joy, fear, and sadness. Through the psalms we can also thank God, praise him, and ask him for his mercy and help.

Songs for God
The psalms were meant to be sung. Much of the original music has been forgotten, but people still sing the psalms today. Here are some verses you might have heard before.

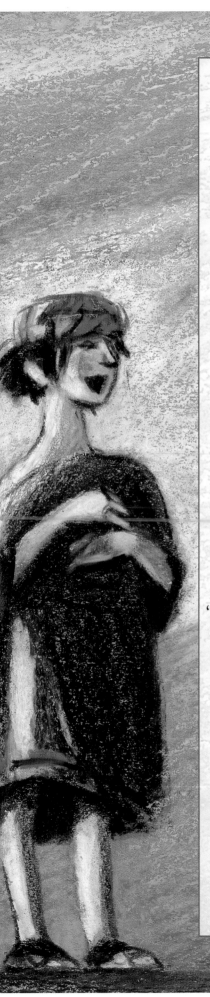

God is great
"The Lord, the Most High, is awesome,
a great king over all the earth."

Psalm 47

Thank you
"You knitted me together in my mother's womb.
I praise you, for I am wondrously made.
Wonderful are your works!"

Psalm 139
"I sought the Lord, and he answered me,
and delivered me from all my fears."

Psalm 34

Forgive me
"Against you, you only, have I sinned,
and done that which is evil in your sight."

Psalm 51

Please help me!
"Be a rock of refuge for me,
a strong fortress to save me!"

Psalm 31
"Guard me, O Lord, from the hands of the wicked;
preserve me from violent men."

Psalm 140
"Be not far from me,
for trouble is near
and there is none to help."

Psalm 22

God, I trust in you!
"You show me the path of life."

Psalm 16
"Those who seek him shall praise the LORD!
May your hearts live for ever!"

Psalm 22

27

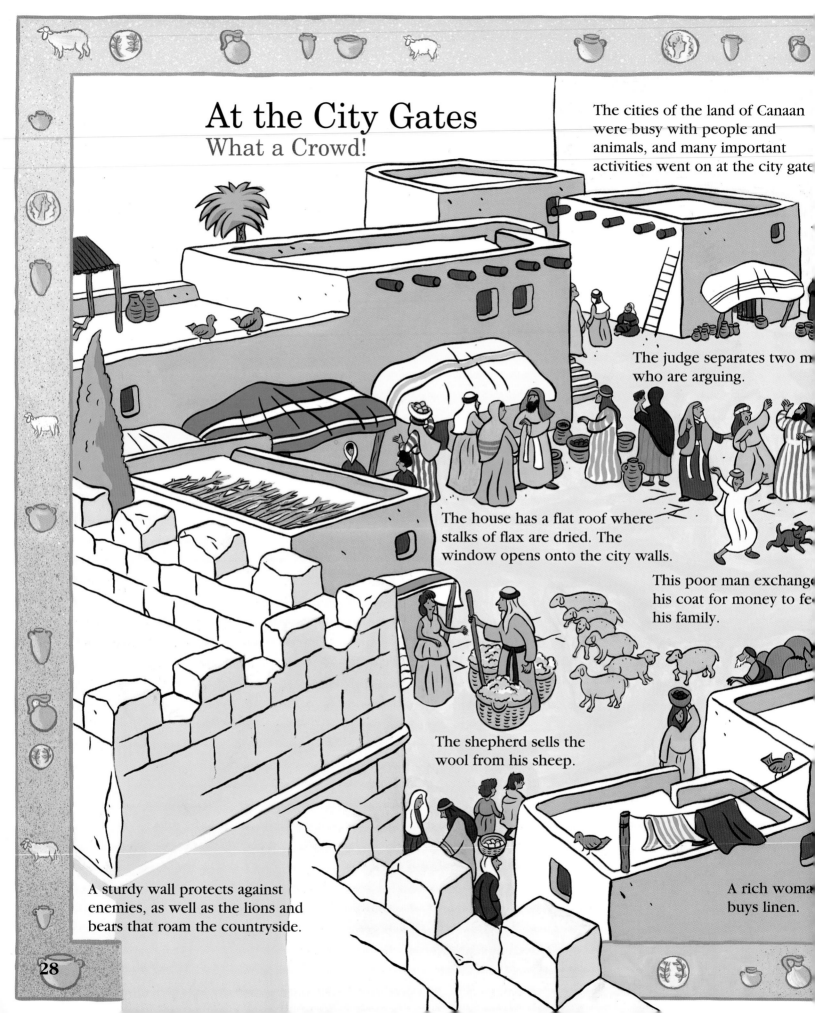

At the City Gates
What a Crowd!

The cities of the land of Canaan were busy with people and animals, and many important activities went on at the city gate

The judge separates two m who are arguing.

The house has a flat roof where stalks of flax are dried. The window opens onto the city walls.

This poor man exchang his coat for money to fe his family.

The shepherd sells the wool from his sheep.

A sturdy wall protects against enemies, as well as the lions and bears that roam the countryside.

A rich woma buys linen.

You must pay a toll to enter the city.

Merchants come to the banker to change money.

The caravan unloads its merchandise.

This merchant sells honey. That was all there was to sweeten food because there was no sugar!

A blind man begs for coins to feed himself.

Pottery and leather sandals are for sale at the market.

Elijah
A Great Prophet

After the reigns of David and his son Solomon, the kingdom of Israel was governed by men who disobeyed God. King Ahab worshipped Baal, the god of storms, and led his people to do wicked things to please this false god. So God sent his prophet Elijah to speak to him.

Trust in God for everything

Elijah went to see Ahab and said, "God is going to punish you if you go on worshipping Baal. There won't be a single drop of rain for years." The king was furious, and Elijah fled far away into the countryside. Then the drought began.

One day, God ordered Elijah to go to the village of Zarephath. There he asked a very poor woman to feed him. All she had was a handful of flour and a little oil. He asked her to bake him some bread, saying, "In the name of the Lord, you shall want for nothing." The woman trusted him. The next day, as though by a miracle, her jar of flour and her pitcher of oil were full again! Though they had enough to eat, the woman's son became very ill and died. Elijah stretched himself over the boy three times and prayed very hard, "Lord, bring this

The prophets

The prophets were men sent by God to speak to the people in his name. They were often despised for saying things people did not want to hear. In the Bible, the prophet Jeremiah foretold misfortunes for those who would not change their hearts. The prophets Amos and Micah criticized those who mistreated the poor. Isaiah and Ezekiel promised that those who suffered would be consoled. Isaiah also told of a savior-king whom God would send to all mankind—the Messiah, which means "the Anointed".

child back to life!" The child revived! Overjoyed, the mother said to Elijah, "You are a man of God!"

The contest on Mount Carmel

A little while later, Elijah returned to see King Ahab. He was still furious: "You prophet of doom!" But Elijah was undaunted. "It is you who brought these troubles on your people by worshipping Baal! Meet me on top of Mount Carmel with your many prophets. Then we'll see who is the one and only God." On the mountain, the king's prophets begged Baal to set fire to an altar of wood, but nothing happened. Elijah made fun of them, "Cry louder! Perhaps he's busy or away on a journey! Or perhaps he's asleep!" Then Elijah prepared an altar and prayed to God to ignite it. In one bolt of lightning, the wood caught fire. There was the proof that Baal did not exist and that God is the master of all! Then the drought ended; the rains came and watered the land once again.

Elijah goes to heaven

Years went by. Elijah met Elisha, whom God had chosen to succeed him as prophet. Now that Elijah's mission had been accomplished, God took him up to himself in a chariot of fire that disappeared into the sky.

A still, small voice

Elijah had to flee for his life. He hid in a cave, where he experienced a roaring wind, an earthquake, and a fire. God was not in any of these, but revealed himself in a still, small voice.

Jonah
A Very Stubborn Prophet

Jonah, go tell the people of Nineveh that God has had enough of their wickedness.

Those cursed foreigners? I'd rather go anywhere but there!

Jonah boarded a foreign ship bound in the opposite direction. The ship was caught in a storm.

God of the Greeks, save us!

God of the Persians, save us!

God of Egypt, save us!

It's my fault. I disobeyed the God of Israel. Throw me overboard!

It's so dark in here. My God, come and save me!

After three days, Jonah was spat back out on the shore. And this time, he went to Nineveh.

Change your hearts! Stop your wickedness, or the city will be destroyed!

The people listened, and even the king repented.

He's right. Let's ask God for forgiveness.

Look, Jonah, they are sorry for their sins. I will forgive them.

The Destruction of Jerusalem
The Babylonian Exile

In Jerusalem, in the year 587 B.C., the young King Zedekiah rebelled against Nebuchadnezzar, the powerful king of Babylon who had conquered Israel. Nebuchadnezzar decided to take revenge on Zedekiah.

The flight from Jerusalem

I was ten years old when the Babylonian army laid siege to Jerusalem. We were completely surrounded with no way in or out! After six months, the bread was all gone, and there was hardly any more water. One night, our army made a hole in the city walls. The soldiers and the king were able to escape, but we were abandoned.

The Babylonian soldiers entered the city. Their cries of victory rang through the streets. They went up to the house of God, the Temple. They took away all the valuables, the gold and the bronze, and then set the Temple on fire. When we saw the flames, we broke out in sobs. My grandfather said he'd rather have been dead than see such a thing. When the fire reached the king's palace and the houses, we realized that the whole city would be burned down.

In panic, we ran out of the city. Several thousand of us watched in horror as Jerusalem went up in flames!

The Babylonians took us prisoner. The next day, King Zedekiah was caught. His sons were killed in front of him. The Babylonians gouged out his eyes and shackled him in chains to be taken to Babylon.

Exiles in Babylon

Babylon! That's where we were taken by force. My grandfather was angry with Zedekiah. He said all of our miseries were his fault! The king had stopped believing in God and had sent away God's messengers, the prophets. In Babylon, we settled on the banks of the great Euphrates River. After fifty-five years, the king of Persia took power. He gave us permission to go back to our homeland. So, with my children and my grandchildren, I was at last able to return to the Promised Land. And I truly hope to end my days there in peace!

The Temple

The Temple was the house of God, where the Ark of the Covenant was kept. When the Hebrews were in the desert, they built a tent for the Ark. In Jerusalem, Solomon built the glorious Temple, where priests offered sacrifices in thanksgiving to God and to ask his forgiveness for the sins of his people.

God's Faithfulness
From Creation to the Birth of Jesus

Hundreds and hundreds of years went by between the creation of the world and the birth of Jesus, but God never abandoned mankind. He established with men a covenant of love, which he renewed over and over again.

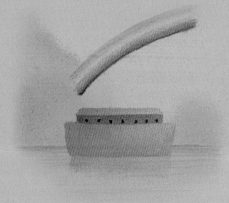

1. God created the earth and the sky and all that lives in them. God created man and woman in his image.

2. God said to Noah, "I set a rainbow in the clouds as the sign of my covenant with all those who live on the earth."

3. "Leave your country and go to the land that I will show you." "I will make a covenant with you and your children, who will be as numerous as the stars in the sky."

4. God said to Moses, "I AM WHO I AM."

5. "I have seen the suffering of my people. I will take them out of Egypt."

6. "This is my covenant with you: I am the Lord your God. I give you commandments to teach you how to love me and one another."

7. David said to Goliath, "My strength is the Lord."

8. God was not in the wind or the earthquake but in a still small voice.

9. God said to Jonah, "Go tell the people of Nineveh: Forty days more and Nineveh will be destroyed!"

10. "Disaster! Our city was destroyed, and we were taken prisoner to Babylon."

11. "The one who is coming is mightier than I. I am not worthy to untie his sandals."

John the Baptist
The Forerunner of Christ

The Hebrew people came to be known as the Jews. They were awaiting the Messiah, the Christ, the promised Savior foretold by the prophets. Many prepared to welcome him at his coming.

Get ready for the Savior!

In those days, there was a man who lived and prayed in the desert. His name was John. He wore a tunic made of camel hair. He ate locusts and wild honey. The words he spoke came from God, for he was a prophet. Great crowds came to listen to him, and he told them to get ready for the Savior: "Change your hearts, change your lives! The Lord is coming; prepare the way for him."

Many deeply wished to reform their lives, and they confessed their sins. John baptized them in the waters of the Jordan River, and their souls were washed clean. For these men and women, this baptism was the beginning of a brand-new life.

Mightier than I

John also said, "I am only a prophet. The one who is coming after me is mightier than I. His sandals I am not worthy to untie. I baptize you with water, but he will baptize you with the Holy Spirit."

The baptism of Jesus

One day, Jesus came to John and asked to be baptized like the others. When John saw him he said, "Behold the Lamb of God, who takes away the sins of the world." After John baptized Jesus, the skies opened and a voice was heard saying, "You are my beloved Son, with whom I am well pleased."

The word *baptism* comes from a Greek word meaning "immersion". The word *Christ* is also Greek. Like the Hebrew word *Messiah*, it means "anointed".

39

The Holy Land
Where the Son of God Came to Meet Us

Jesus walked with his friends, called disciples, from village to village, across the whole country. Wherever they went, they healed the sick and preached the good news of God's love and mercy. Life there was sometimes difficult: the land was occupied by the powerful Romans.

Not everyone believed Jesus

In the Temple in Jerusalem, the Jewish priests offered sacrifices for the people to God. Throughout the country, Jews also gathered in houses of prayer, or synagogues, to read the Scriptures and to pray. Jesus preached and healed in the Temple and in the synagogues. The Jewish religious leaders, who were divided into groups such as the Sadducees and Pharisees, often quarreled with Jesus. They saw Jesus perform miracles and heard him proclaim the love of God, yet many accused Jesus of disobeying the laws of their religion. Many did not believe that Jesus was the Son of God.

Caesar

SAMARIA

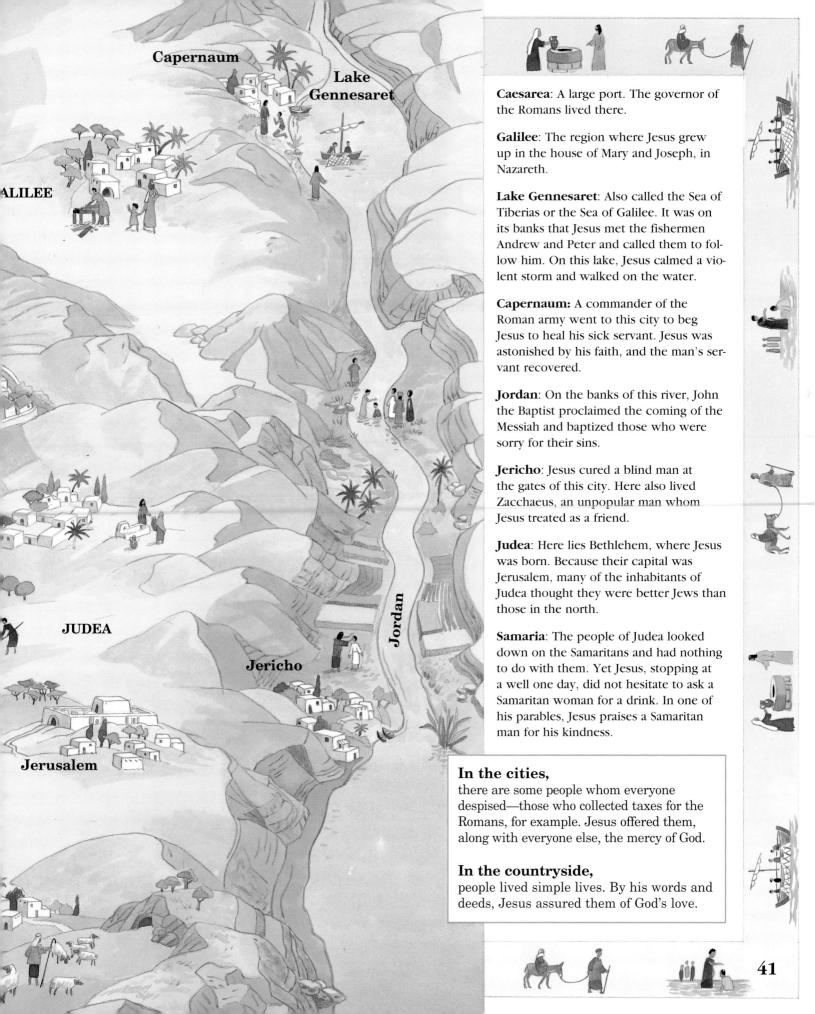

Caesarea: A large port. The governor of the Romans lived there.

Galilee: The region where Jesus grew up in the house of Mary and Joseph, in Nazareth.

Lake Gennesaret: Also called the Sea of Tiberias or the Sea of Galilee. It was on its banks that Jesus met the fishermen Andrew and Peter and called them to follow him. On this lake, Jesus calmed a violent storm and walked on the water.

Capernaum: A commander of the Roman army went to this city to beg Jesus to heal his sick servant. Jesus was astonished by his faith, and the man's servant recovered.

Jordan: On the banks of this river, John the Baptist proclaimed the coming of the Messiah and baptized those who were sorry for their sins.

Jericho: Jesus cured a blind man at the gates of this city. Here also lived Zacchaeus, an unpopular man whom Jesus treated as a friend.

Judea: Here lies Bethlehem, where Jesus was born. Because their capital was Jerusalem, many of the inhabitants of Judea thought they were better Jews than those in the north.

Samaria: The people of Judea looked down on the Samaritans and had nothing to do with them. Yet Jesus, stopping at a well one day, did not hesitate to ask a Samaritan woman for a drink. In one of his parables, Jesus praises a Samaritan man for his kindness.

In the cities,
there are some people whom everyone despised—those who collected taxes for the Romans, for example. Jesus offered them, along with everyone else, the mercy of God.

In the countryside,
people lived simple lives. By his words and deeds, Jesus assured them of God's love.

41

Jesus
A Baby in a Manger

God had promised to send the Savior, and many of his friends were awaiting this event. Among them was a girl named Mary who received a most surprising visit.

The annunciation to Mary

God sent the angel Gabriel to a girl named Mary. She lived in the town of Nazareth in Galilee and was engaged to Joseph of the family of King David.

"Hail, Mary, full of grace. The Lord is with you!" said the angel.

Mary was astonished!

"Do not be afraid, Mary. You will have a son, and you shall name him Jesus. He will be a great king forever."

Mary replied, "But how can that be? I'm not married yet."

"The Holy Spirit will come upon you, and the power of God will overshadow you. This is why the child will be called the Son of God!"

Mary said, "I am here to serve the Lord. Let it be to me as you say." And the angel left her.

Born in Bethlehem

After this, the Roman emperor ordered a census to be taken to count all his subjects. Each man had to register his family in the town where he was born. So Joseph set out for Bethlehem with his wife, Mary, who was with child. When they arrived, Mary gave birth to her baby. She wrapped him in swaddling cloths and laid him in a manger, because there was no room for them at the inn.

The shepherds and the magi

Shepherds were guarding their flocks nearby. Suddenly, they were surrounded by light, and an angel said to them, "I bring you good news of great joy! Today the Savior is born. You will find him in Bethlehem, lying in a manger." The shepherds said to each other, "Quick, let's go see this child!"

In a faraway land, wise men called magi saw a special star. They set off and followed it until they reached Bethlehem. There they bowed down before the baby Jesus and offered him gifts.

Mary, Joseph, and Jesus settled in Nazareth. Joseph worked as a carpenter, and Jesus grew in strength and wisdom.

Finding Jesus in the Temple

When Jesus was twelve years old, he went with Mary and Joseph on pilgrimage to Jerusalem. On their way home, Mary and Joseph realized that Jesus was missing. So they went back in search of him. At last, they found Jesus in the Temple, asking the religious scholars questions. Mary asked, "Son, why have you done this to us?" Jesus answered, "Why were you looking for me? Didn't you know that I had to be in my Father's house?"

Jesus
All Kinds of Friends

After his baptism, Jesus prayed and fasted for forty days in the desert. Then he began to travel the country, performing miracles and announcing that God is our Father, who loves and forgives us. Some of those who met Jesus followed him and became his friends.

Peter
"Jesus called us."
I was fishing on the lake with my brother Andrew. Jesus passed by and said to us, "Follow me, and I will make you fishers of men." We didn't really understand what Jesus meant, but there was something about him that made us leave everything to follow him.

John
"He reveals God."
I often sat by Jesus' side and listened carefully to what he said. One day, Jesus led Peter, James, and me to the top of a mountain. There he was trans-

formed before our eyes: his face became as dazzling as the sun. Then a voice came from heaven, saying, "This is my beloved Son. Listen to him."

Mary Magdalene
"He changed my life."

Before I met Jesus, my life was dark and empty. I was alone and friendless. When I heard the words of Jesus, I was overwhelmed: he spoke about the love of God like no one else. I went to see him; he didn't judge me. He saw the love that was in the depths of my heart, and he freed me from everything that held me back from God. I followed him right to the end. I was there when they nailed him to the Cross, and I was the first one to discover the empty tomb. He appeared to me first, and I ran to tell our friends, "I've seen the Lord! He is risen!"

The Twelve

Jesus chose twelve men to be his apostles, those with whom he would share his mission in a particular way. These are their names: Andrew and his brother Simon Peter, James and his brother John, Philip and his friend Bartholomew (also called Nathanael), Thomas, Matthew the evangelist, another James, Jude, Simon, and Judas.

Jesus
Encounters that Changed Everything

Jesus never stopped traveling, and his disciples followed him. Wherever Jesus went, crowds of people flocked to him. He cured diseases, forgave sins, and had compassion for the poor. He even raised the dead. For all those who met Jesus, life would never be the same again.

Zacchaeus
"Jesus shows kindness to sinners."
I'm so short that I had to climb a tree to see Jesus in the crowd. He saw me and said, "Zacchaeus, let me come and stay at your house." There was nasty grumbling: "How scandalous! He's going to that thief's house!" But I was so happy that I made him a promise: "I will give half of my possessions to the poor. And if I have stolen from anyone, I will pay it back four times over."

Bartimaeus
"Jesus gives sight to the blind."
"There's Jesus! There's Jesus!" shouted the crowd. And I, blind Bartimaeus, started to call out to him, "Jesus, please, have mercy on me!" People told me to be quiet, but I believed that Jesus could restore my sight. So I kept on shouting. Jesus heard me and

had me brought to him. "What do you want me to do for you?" he asked. "I want to see!" He said, "Go, your faith has saved you." Then my eyes were opened, and I could see!

Martha
"Jesus taught me to worry less and listen to God more."

When Jesus came to our house in Bethany, my sister, Mary, sat next to him, listening without a care in the world! I got angry: "She could at least give me a hand!" But Jesus said, "You are so busy and worried about many things, but there are much more important things than fixing dinner. Mary has chosen to listen to me; leave her be!"

Nicodemus
"Jesus gives new life."

I, a Pharisee, spoke to Jesus secretly during the night: God has sent you to us." Jesus said, "No one can see the Kingdom of God without being born anew."

Lazarus
"Jesus is more powerful than death."

I became very ill and died. My sisters, Martha and Mary, believed that Jesus could have healed me if he had come in time. When he arrived, Mary said, "Lord, if you had been here, Lazarus wouldn't have died!" Jesus wept. Then he had my tomb opened and said, "Lazarus, come out!" Although dead, I heard him and got up. Everyone there was amazed and understood that Jesus was stronger than death.

The Parables of Jesus
Simple but Wise Stories

To help his friends understand the love of God, Jesus told them simple stories.

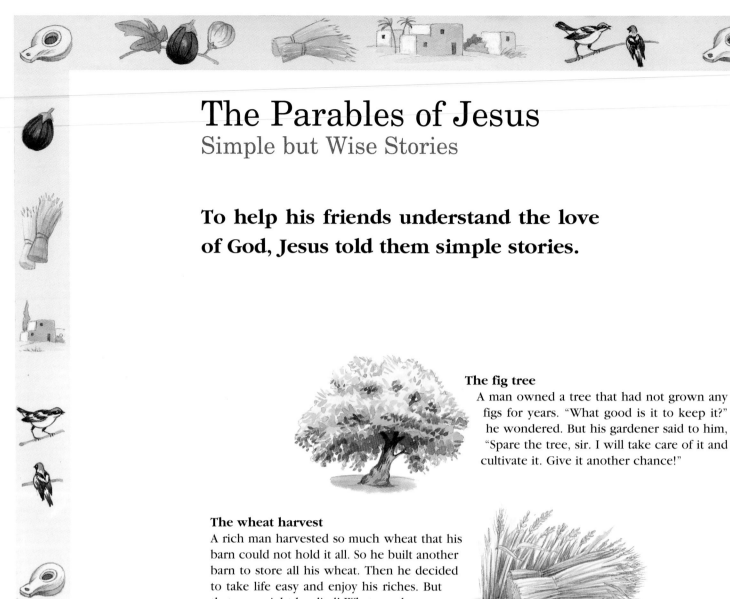

The fig tree

A man owned a tree that had not grown any figs for years. "What good is it to keep it?" he wondered. But his gardener said to him, "Spare the tree, sir. I will take care of it and cultivate it. Give it another chance!"

The wheat harvest

A rich man harvested so much wheat that his barn could not hold it all. So he built another barn to store all his wheat. Then he decided to take life easy and enjoy his riches. But that very night he died! What good were all of his riches then?

The lamp

A lamp is made to light up a house. No one lights a lamp and puts it under a bed; instead he puts the lamp on a stand, where it can help everyone to see.

The good Samaritan

Once there was a traveler who was attacked by bandits, who left him for dead. Two very religious men passed by but did not stop to help him. Finally a man from Samaria took pity on the injured man. He stopped and treated his wounds with wine and oil and put him on his donkey. He took the man to an inn and gave the innkeeper two silver coins to take care of him.

The lost sheep

God is like a shepherd who owns a hundred sheep. When one of them strays into the mountains, he leaves the ninety-nine other sheep to go in search of the one that is lost. What rejoicing when he finds it!

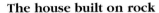

The house built on rock

He who hears my words, said Jesus, and acts on them is like a man who built his house on solid rock; nothing can destroy that house. But he who hears me and does not change his life is like a man who built his house on sand; the slightest storm will knock that house down.

The seed that becomes a tree

The Kingdom of heaven is like a mustard seed that a man planted. It is the tiniest of seeds, but when it grows, it becomes a great tree in which birds build their nests.

The hidden treasure

The Kingdom of heaven is like a hidden treasure that a man finds in a field. He sells all that he has to buy that field.

The sower

A sower went out to plant seeds. Some seeds fell on the path, and birds came and ate them up. Some fell on rocky ground: they sprouted too fast and withered. Others fell among thorns that choked the young plants. But others fell on good soil, and they produced grain. The seed is the Word of God, and the good soil is the heart of him who hears God's word and puts it into practice.

The fearful servant

Before leaving on a journey, a wealthy man entrusted his money to his servants. When he returned, his servants told him about the profits they had made with his money. One servant, however, had hidden the money because he was afraid his actions might displease his master. The master was very disappointed with this servant, who did not trust him enough to do his best.

A Great Parable
A Father and His Two Sons

Here is one of the most beloved stories of Jesus. Sometimes called "The Prodigal Son", it tells us about God's mercy.
A father had two sons. One day, the younger son said:

Father, give me my share of your money. Right away!

Then he left for a faraway land.

We're rich and young! Let's have fun!

When he had spent all his money, there was a great famine in the land.

Do you have any work for me?

Go tend my pigs.

Back home, my father's workers have nice bread to eat. But here, even the pigs eat better than I do.

I'll go back home to my father. I will be his hired hand.

My son! My son!

Jesus Speaks about the Father
The Good News of God's Love

Jesus proclaimed good news: God loves us the way a good father loves his children.

Jesus said that God is our Father who loves us so much that we can ask him for what we need and desire: "Ask, and it will be given to you; seek, and you shall find; knock, and it will be opened to you. For everyone who asks receives; and he who seeks, finds, and to him who knocks it will be opened."

Someone said to Jesus, "Lord, show us the Father, and we will be satisfied." Jesus replied, "He who has seen me has seen the Father.... Believe me that I am in the Father and the Father is in me."

One day, children gathered around Jesus. Someone said, "Go away! You're bothering Jesus!" But Jesus said, "Let the children come to me. Do not stop them. Those who trust in me as these children do will enter the Kingdom of heaven." And he picked up the children and blessed them.

Jesus said to his followers: "As the Father has loved me, so have I loved you; abide in my love. If you keep my commandments, you will abide in my love.
. . . And this is my commandment, that you love one another as I have loved you."

Can we see God?

No, God is pure spirit, so we cannot see him. But we can see what God does. We can see the beautiful world he has made. We can see his fatherly love in all the things our family provides for us. And most of all, we can see God by looking at what Jesus did and listening to what he said.

The Our Father
The Prayer of Jesus

The friends of Jesus asked him, "Lord, teach us to pray." And he taught them this beautiful prayer to God, addressing him as Father. It is the great prayer of Christians, which we still say today, just as Jesus taught us.

Our Father, who art in heaven,

Hallowed be thy name.

Thy kingdom come.

Thy will be done,

On earth as it is in heaven.

Give us this day our daily bread;

And forgive us our trespasses

As we forgive those who trespass against us;

And lead us not into temptation,

But deliver us from evil.

The Last Supper
Jesus' Farewell Meal

Jesus went up to Jerusalem to celebrate the Passover. Seated on a donkey, he rode into the city to the cries of his countrymen: "Hosanna! Blessed is he who comes in the name of the Lord! Hosanna in the highest!" Jesus' enemies were furious.

Passover

Each spring, Jews celebrate the Passover. They eat a special meal with unleavened bread. They read from Exodus, which tells how God sent Moses to save their ancestors from slavery in Egypt. They sing psalms and give thanks to God.

Judas' betrayal

The religious leaders wanted to kill Jesus. Judas, one of the Twelve, offered to betray him for thirty silver coins.

Jesus shares his life

On Thursday during the season of Passover, Jesus gathered with his disciples for a farewell meal. He knew he was about to die. He took bread and gave thanks to God. Then he broke the bread and gave it to his disciples, saying, "Take this and eat of it, for this is my Body, which will be given up for you." Then he took the chalice of wine, gave thanks to God, and gave it to them, saying, "Take this and drink from it, for this is the chalice of my Blood, the

Blood of the new and eternal covenant, which will be poured out for you and for many for the forgiveness of sins. Do this in memory of me."

Jesus, the servant

After the meal, Jesus said, "Whoever wishes to be great among you must be your servant. I did not come to be served but to serve, and to give my life." Then Jesus got up from the table and tied a towel around his waist. He poured water into a basin. He washed his friends' feet and dried them with the towel as a servant would. Peter refused: "Lord, you will never wash my feet!" Jesus answered, "Afterward you will understand." Then Jesus said to his friends, "What I have done for you, you too must do for others."

Jesus and his apostles go out into the night

Jesus and his apostles left for the garden of Gethsemane. On the way, Jesus said, "This very night you will all abandon me." Peter cried out, "I will never abandon you." Jesus replied, "I tell you, Peter, this night, before the cock crows, you will deny me three times."

The Crucifixion
Jesus Dies for Us

Judas told the religious leaders where to find Jesus. They had Jesus arrested and tried him like a criminal. Jesus was condemned to die and was crucified.

Alone with God

Jesus and his friends arrived at the garden of Gethsemane. Jesus was afraid: "I am sorrowful to the point of death. Stay awake and pray with me!" But the apostles fell asleep, and Jesus was left alone with God. Judas arrived with armed men. He approached Jesus and, as a signal to the armed men, kissed him. Then the men seized Jesus and led him away.

Judged and beaten

Jesus was judged by the Jewish leaders. They asked him, "Are you the Son of God?" Jesus answered, "I am." They were horrified: "How dare this man claim to be equal to God! He deserves to die." On Friday morning, they took Jesus to the Roman governor, Pontius Pilate, and demanded his death. Those standing by in a crowd screamed, "Crucify him!" So Pilate condemned Jesus to death. Roman soldiers flogged Jesus. They placed a scarlet robe on him and put a crown of thorns on his head. They mocked him, saying, "Hail, King of the Jews!"

Peter's denial

Peter approached the place where Jesus was being tried. Someone recognized him and said, "You're one of Jesus' followers!" Peter was frightened: "No, I'm not!" Two more times he was accused of being a disciple of Jesus, and two more times he swore he did not know him. Then he heard a cock crow and, remembering what Jesus had said, broke down in sobs.

Nailed to the Cross

The soldiers led Jesus outside the city walls, where they nailed him to the Cross. Two thieves were also crucified, one on either side of Jesus. His Mother, Mary, and John and Mary Magdalene stood at the foot of the Cross. Some onlookers scoffed: "Let him save himself if he's really the Son of God!" Jesus said, "Father, forgive them, for they know not what they do." One of the thieves defended Jesus, saying, "He has done nothing wrong!" Jesus said to him, "Today you will be with me in paradise." Suddenly, the sky darkened. Jesus gave a great cry and said, "Father, into your hands I commend my spirit!" Then he died. A soldier nearby exclaimed, "Truly this was the Son of God!" Jesus' friends took his body, wrapped it in linen, and laid it in a tomb carved out of rock.

The Cross

Death on a cross was the most horrible and most shameful form of execution imaginable in the time of Jesus. It was the death penalty reserved for criminals and rebels. Jesus carried the Cross on his shoulders until the soldiers, seeing that he was unable to carry it by himself, ordered a passerby, Simon of Cyrene, to carry it for him.

The Resurrection
Jesus Is Alive!

Jesus died on Friday, and his friends laid his body in a tomb. When some women went to the tomb on Sunday morning, Jesus was not there. He had risen from the dead!

The burial of Jesus

After Jesus had died, he needed to be buried quickly because the Sabbath, the day of the week Jews honor God by resting from their work, began at sundown. Since the women did not have time to bathe and anoint the body of Jesus properly, they returned with spices on Sunday. To celebrate the Resurrection, Sunday became the day of worship for Christians.

Where is Jesus?

Early on Sunday morning, Mary Magdalene and some other women went to anoint Jesus' body with spices. What a surprise: the stone that had closed the tomb had been rolled away, and the body of Jesus was gone!

Two angels stood before the women and said, "Why are you looking for Jesus among the dead? He is alive! He is not here; he is risen!" The women ran quickly to announce the news. But nobody believed them! Mary Magdalene returned to the tomb with Peter and John. Seeing that Jesus was gone, the apostles went to tell others. Then the risen Lord appeared to Mary.

The stranger on the road

Later on, two of Jesus' friends were talking as they walked toward the village of Emmaus. A man joined them and walked along with them. It was Jesus, but they did not recognize him.

Jesus asked them, "What were you talking about?" They stopped and, looking sad, said, "You must be the only one who hasn't heard what things have happened in Jerusalem these last days!" Jesus asked, "What things?" And they told Jesus everything about him. "We were so disappointed," they continued, "because we had hoped Jesus would save our nation. What's more, this morning some women went to the tomb and found it empty. Angels told them that Jesus is alive." Jesus said, "How slow of heart you are to believe! The prophets had foretold these things!" Then Jesus explained everything that was written about him in the Scriptures.

We recognized him!

Soon the men arrived at the village. It seemed as if Jesus would continue on his way, so they asked him, "Stay with us, for it is getting late." As they began dinner, Jesus took the bread, broke it, and gave it to them. In that moment, they recognized him, but Jesus vanished. The two friends said to each other, "It was Jesus! When he talked to us on the road, didn't our hearts burn with joy?" Without losing a moment, they returned to Jerusalem to announce that they had recognized the risen Lord in the breaking of the bread.

Pentecost
The Coming of the Holy Spirit

After the Resurrection, Jesus appeared many times to his friends to show them that he was alive. Before returning to the Father, Jesus told his apostles to continue his mission throughout the world. He promised that they would receive the help of the Holy Spirit.

An event that creates a sensation

On Pentecost, the city of Jerusalem was crowded. Jewish pilgrims had come from all over to celebrate God's giving the Ten Commandments to Moses. Jesus' apostles were gathered together with his Mother in a house. Suddenly, there came a loud noise like that of a mighty wind. Those who were there saw what looked like tongues of fire coming down upon them. With that, they were all filled with the Holy Spirit. They could no longer contain their joy and began proclaiming the wonderful news about Jesus.

On hearing the commotion, a great crowd gathered around the house. Among them were

The Ascension

The risen Jesus led his friends up a mountain and said to them, "I am returning to my Father. You shall be my witnesses here and everywhere, to the ends of the earth." When he had said this, he was taken up into the sky before their very eyes. A cloud came and hid him from view. His friends searched the sky, speechless with amazement! Then two men dressed in white appeared and said to them, "Why do you stand there looking up to heaven?" So Jesus' friends returned to Jerusalem.

62

people from many lands, but each of them heard the apostles speaking in his own language. "It's incredible!" the people said. "These men are from Galilee, yet we all hear them speaking in our own languages. What can this mean?" Others snickered, saying, "They've drunk too much wine."

A speech that turns the world upside down

Then Peter addressed the crowd: "People of this land, and you others visiting Jerusalem, listen to me! No, we are not drunk! It's something else: Jesus, whom God sent you, who worked wonders and signs among you, whom you crucified—God has raised him from the dead. Yes, of this we are witnesses! He received the Holy Spirit from the Father and has sent this Spirit to us today. Yes, Jesus is the Lord, the Christ." Many in the crowd were cut to the heart and asked Peter, "What are we to do?" He answered them, "Repent and be baptized for the forgiveness of your sins, and you shall receive the Holy Spirit." That day, three thousand people were baptized.

In the Power of the Spirit
The Adventures of the First Believers

After the apostles received the Holy Spirit, they went out to announce everywhere that Jesus was the promised Messiah.

What I do have, I give to you!

In Jerusalem, the first believers gathered to pray and to break bread as Jesus had shown them. They shared all their money and their homes with each other. They went to the Temple every day to pray. One afternoon, when Peter and John were entering the Temple, a lame beggar asked them for money. Peter said to him, "I have no money. But I will give you what I do have. In the name of Jesus Christ, rise and walk!" Peter took him by the hand, and he stood up and walked.

Stephen forgives his enemies

A Christian named Stephen was known for the wonders he worked in the name of God. His enemies had him brought before the court. Stephen spoke so well that the jealous mob started to stone him. Stephen prayed, "Lord Jesus, receive my spirit." As he died, he said, "Lord, do not hold this sin against them."

Peter and John in prison

The men who had had Jesus killed also had Peter, John, and their friends arrested. They were thrown into prison. But one night, an angel came to open the prison doors and set them free. Their enemies were so angry that they had them arrested again. Peter was unafraid and cried out, "We must obey God rather than men!" They were all whipped and then released.

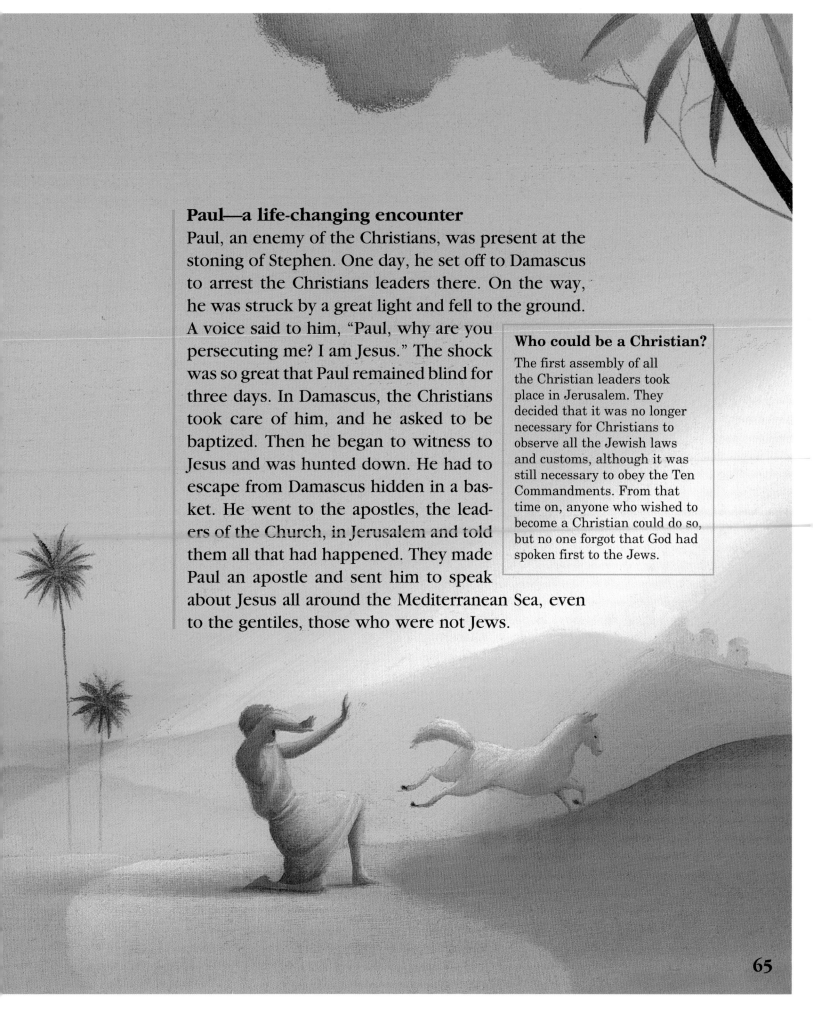

Paul—a life-changing encounter

Paul, an enemy of the Christians, was present at the stoning of Stephen. One day, he set off to Damascus to arrest the Christians leaders there. On the way, he was struck by a great light and fell to the ground. A voice said to him, "Paul, why are you persecuting me? I am Jesus." The shock was so great that Paul remained blind for three days. In Damascus, the Christians took care of him, and he asked to be baptized. Then he began to witness to Jesus and was hunted down. He had to escape from Damascus hidden in a basket. He went to the apostles, the leaders of the Church, in Jerusalem and told them all that had happened. They made Paul an apostle and sent him to speak about Jesus all around the Mediterranean Sea, even to the gentiles, those who were not Jews.

Who could be a Christian?

The first assembly of all the Christian leaders took place in Jerusalem. They decided that it was no longer necessary for Christians to observe all the Jewish laws and customs, although it was still necessary to obey the Ten Commandments. From that time on, anyone who wished to become a Christian could do so, but no one forgot that God had spoken first to the Jews.

Paul
The Tireless Traveler

For twenty years, Paul traveled the roads going from city to city to make Jesus known. So many adventures and dangers along the way, and so many meetings with friends!

Philippi

Rome

Rome: This is where Paul and Peter were martyred around the year 64.

Athens: For the most part, neither the Jews nor the gentiles of Athens understood Paul when he told them about Jesus and the Resurrection. They made fun of Paul. How discouraging! Yet a few men and women did believe and became Christians.

Athens

Corinth

Corinth: Here Paul made two good friends—Aquila and his wife, Priscilla—and baptized many people. Later Paul wrote two famous letters to the Corinthians, in which he begged them to remain faithful to Christ, to show love and forbearance toward one another, and not to break into factions.

Crete

Antioch: The biggest city in the region. It was here that those who believed in Christ were called Christians for the first time.

Philippi: Here Paul and his friend [Si]las baptized a rich merchant named [Ly]dia. The judges of the city had them [wh]ipped and put into prison. God [ca]me to their rescue by opening the [pri]son doors. One of the guards was [so] impressed that he asked to become [a] Christian.

Antioch

Tarsus: Paul was born here and learned his trade as a tentmaker.

Lystra

Tarsus

Ephesus

Lystra: In this city, Paul and his friend Barnabas cured the sick. Some people thought Paul and Barnabas were gods! Other people threw stones at them, and Paul was lucky to escape with his life.

Ephesus: In this city, Demetrius was a maker of statuettes of the goddess Artemis. When Paul told him that one should not make statues of false gods, Demetrius feared he would be ruined. He stirred up a riot against Paul.

Crete: On his way to Rome, Paul was shipwrecked near this large island.

Jerusalem: It was here that Paul was arrested and sent to Rome to be judged by the emperor.

Jerusalem

Witnesses of Christ
Passing on the Faith

Today, two thousand years after the Resurrection, billions of Christians believe that Jesus is the Son of God, who offers mankind a new life full of hope and joy! For this reason, Christians today, like those of the early Church, try to share their faith in Jesus with others.

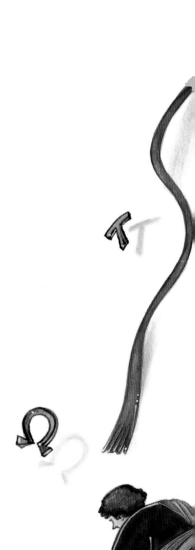

Keeping memories alive

The apostles set off throughout the world to spread the good news about Jesus. They spoke of the things they had seen with their own eyes. All around the Mediterranean Sea, the apostles formed groups of Christians who believed in Jesus based on their testimony and who experienced the power of the Spirit in their lives. Soon countless believers were sharing their newfound faith in Christ. As the apostles grew older and the Church grew larger, it became necessary to write down everything that could be remembered about Jesus.

Four outlooks on Christ

The four Gospels have a lot in common. They all report the main things Jesus said and did. If you look closely, though, you will see that they do not say exactly the same thing. Matthew, Mark, Luke, and John give different outlooks on Jesus. The Church understands that four different points of view are needed to make the fullest possible portrait of Jesus.

Pass it on!

The four Gospels have been passed all the way down to you. In the following pages, you will discover how the Church has handed on the faith, from the time of the apostles to the present day. You are at the receiving end of a long line of witnesses, and now it is your turn to meet Jesus in the Gospels, to believe in him, and to carry on the task of sharing him with others. In that way, those who come after you can believe in Jesus Christ too!

Four Gospels

From all that had been written about Jesus, the Church selected four books: the Gospels. The word *gospel* means "good news" in Greek. The four Gospels were written in Greek, which was the language spoken at the time.

69

2

The Christian Faithful

The History of the Church

Christians in Danger
The Martyrdom of Blandina

In the early years of the Church, many Romans did not like the Christians because they refused to worship the Roman gods and to bow down before the emperor as if he were divine. They were hunted everywhere. One Christian tells what happened in the year 177.

Death to the Christians!

What terrible trials we have just gone through! It all started at the beginning of the summer. On all the street corners, people were yelling, "Death to the Christians!" To calm the crowd, the Roman governor had more than sixty of our friends arrested. He told them they would be sentenced to death if they went on loving Jesus. They didn't even have a chance to defend themselves: the crowd hurled insults, punched them, and threw them to the ground. All those I love took a terrible beating—Attalus, Sanctus and above all Maturus, who had only just been baptized; even old Pothinus, our bishop, who was ninety years old!

The arena is a big open-air circus where the Romans held chariot races and fights to the death. Men fought men and also ferocious animals.

Stronger than the wicked!

They were dragged off to prison. They knew the authorities would try to force them to deny their faith in Jesus Christ. Pothinus was worried. He thought to himself, "Will the youngest ones be able to endure the test? Especially Blandina, who is so frail?" Some stood their ground, but it was so hard; others gave in—but not Blandina! She never stopped repeating, "I am a Christian, and Christians try to do good."

Thrown to the lions

All those who remained steadfast in the faith were taken by the soldiers to the arena to be put to death. Blandina was bound to a stake. She was not afraid; she prayed to the Lord. They let the lions loose, but not one of them dared go near her. The others who were dying heard Blandina's prayer and saw her arms stretched out. She reminded them of how Jesus had died, and it gave them courage. Finally, Blandina was tied up in a net and thrown on the horns of a raging bull. She was the last to die. I'm certain that her prayer was so heartfelt that she didn't feel a thing. She was already with Jesus. How inspiring: it was the littlest one who helped her fellow Christians to be brave to the end!

In the catacombs

At the very beginning, Christians did not have churches; they gathered in the homes of believers. When they were hounded like criminals, they met secretly in hidden places. In Rome, they met in underground cemeteries called catacombs. They prayed together and celebrated Mass near the tombs of their fellow Christians.

Europe Is Christianized
Fearless Voyagers

At first, the early Christians proclaimed Jesus to the Greeks and the Romans around the Mediterranean Sea. Then merchants, soldiers, monks, bishops, priests, and kings spread the Christian faith to all the peoples of Europe.

Saint Columba—Ireland, Gaul, Italy
This monk was a great missionary who left Ireland in the company of a few friends. He crisscrossed Gaul all the way to Italy, founding monasteries along the way.

Saint Patrick—Ireland
At age sixteen, Patrick was captured by pirates and sold as a slave in Ireland. He escaped. He became a bishop and returned to Ireland to teach about Jesus.

Saint Augustine of Canterbury—England
The pope sent Augustine to England to convert the Anglo-Saxons. Augustine built Canterbury Cathedral and its abbey.

Saint Martin—Gaul
This soldier, the son of a Roman, became the bishop of Tours. He founded a monastery and sent out priests to speak of Jesus throughout the countryside.

Saint Leander and Saint Isidore—Spain
These men organized the life of the Church in Spain. Leander became the bishop of Seville. His brother Isidore succeeded him.

Saint Benedict—Italy
Benedict left a worldly life in Rome to devote himself to Jesus. He invented a rule of life for monks with regular times for prayer and work. He founded many monasteries that followed this rule.

Emperor Charlemagne—Europe
A great conqueror, Charlemagne wanted all the people of his empire to be Christian. He was very active: he enacted good laws, built beautiful churches, and promoted scholarship.

Saints Cyril and Methodius—Russia
These two monks spread the name of Jesus to the people of Eastern Europe.
They invented an alphabet to write in the Russian language.

Saint Boniface—Germany
This English monk traveled to Germany to teach the people there about Jesus. He settled in Bavaria.

King Clovis—Gaul*
This king of the mighty Franks became a Christian through the influence of his wife, Saint Clothilde. He was baptized along with all his soldiers. After him, all the kings of France would be Christian.

*Gaul was an ancient region of western Europe, corresponding roughly to the present countries of France and Belgium.

Saint Gregory the Great—Italy
This great pope wished to be the servant of all Christians. He took care of the people of Rome during a famine. He sent missionaries to England. A very beautiful style of singing bears his name: Gregorian chant.

Hugh
A Boy in the Middle Ages

A long time ago, Europe was very different from the way it is today. Almost everyone lived in the country and worked in the fields. Life was hard: wars terrorized the people, and bad harvests brought famine. Hugh, a boy of the Middle Ages, tells his story.

My village

I live in a village in the country. My father is a peasant. He farms Baron Philip's lands and gives him part of the harvest. In exchange, the baron protects us in his castle when enemies come to make war.

I don't go to school. My brothers and I help our father plow the fields and take care of the farm animals. My sisters stay at home to help our mother with her work and look after our youngest siblings.

At Mass

Every Sunday, we go to Mass in the new village church. I like to look at the pictures of the life of Jesus painted on the walls. My favorite is the one of the Nativity. The stable in the picture looks like the one on our farm. It almost looks as if Jesus had been

born at our place! Near the altar is a statue of good Saint Martin. He is much loved in our area. Our village is named after him.

I was baptized a day or two after I was born. It is a custom here to baptize babies when they are very young, because many babies die of sickness. Later, the priest will teach me prayers in Latin, and I'll make my First Communion.

A time for peace

Our bishop, Roger, called all the warlike barons to a meeting and told them, "It is forbidden to make war before Christmas, before Easter, or during the summer. If you disobey and die without repenting, you will go to hell!" They were all frightened. Thanks to the bishop, there are fewer wars and we can get on with our work in peace. The harvest was good last year: we had enough to eat all winter.

Pilgrimages

In the Middle Ages, many European Christians made long trips on foot or on horseback to do penance for their sins. Those who journeyed to holy places were called pilgrims, which comes from the Latin word that means "foreigners". Some went as far as Jerusalem to pray at Christ's tomb, while others travelled to Compostella, Spain, to the burial place of Saint James the apostle.

77

The Monastery
Lives Devoted to Prayer

Many monasteries were built all over Europe in the Middle Ages. Men and women withdrew there to devote their lives entirely to God. Monks and nuns, as they do even today, spent much of their time in prayer, but in the monastery, there was much work to do too. Monasteries much like those in the Middle Ages exist today in many places of the world.

Living together
Monasteries were most often built in quiet places far from the city. Regular times for prayer and work marked the rhythm of the day. Monks and nuns respected certain regulations called the Rule. A leader (an abbot or abbess) was chosen by the members of the order to be in charge of the monastery for a certain period.

The cells were very small private bedrooms. The monks slept there of course, but they also went there to pray in solitude.

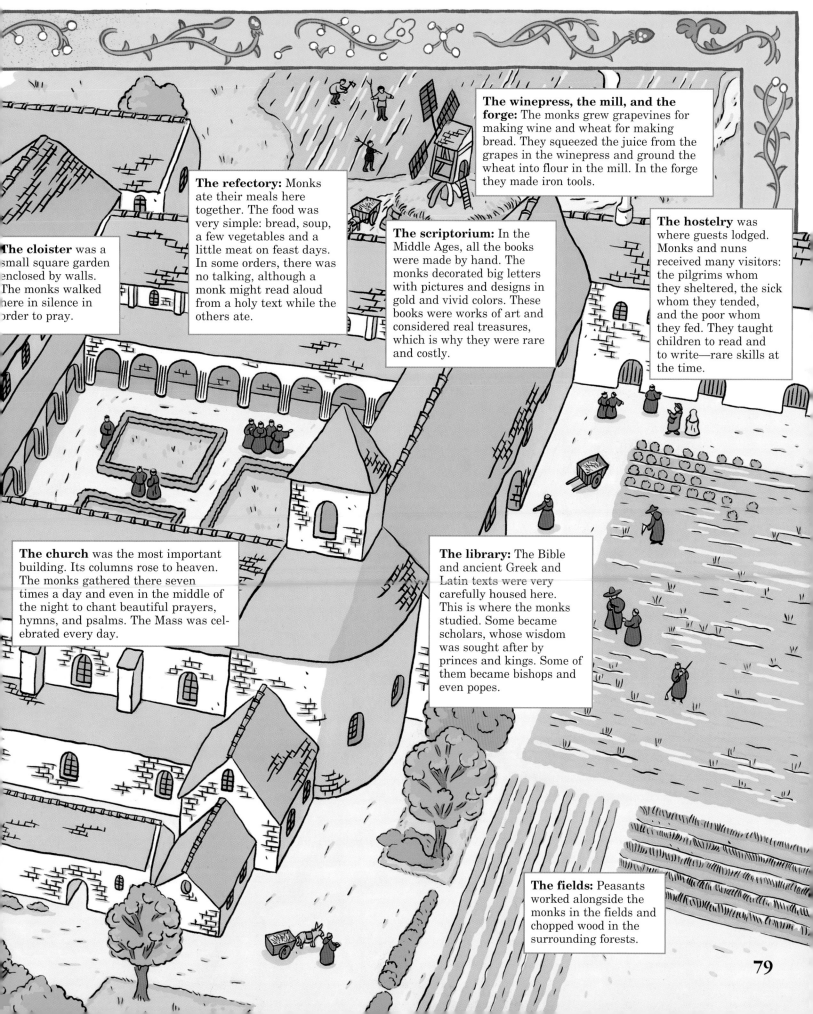

The winepress, the mill, and the forge: The monks grew grapevines for making wine and wheat for making bread. They squeezed the juice from the grapes in the winepress and ground the wheat into flour in the mill. In the forge they made iron tools.

The refectory: Monks ate their meals here together. The food was very simple: bread, soup, a few vegetables and a little meat on feast days. In some orders, there was no talking, although a monk might read aloud from a holy text while the others ate.

The cloister was a small square garden enclosed by walls. The monks walked here in silence in order to pray.

The scriptorium: In the Middle Ages, all the books were made by hand. The monks decorated big letters with pictures and designs in gold and vivid colors. These books were works of art and considered real treasures, which is why they were rare and costly.

The hostelry was where guests lodged. Monks and nuns received many visitors: the pilgrims whom they sheltered, the sick whom they tended, and the poor whom they fed. They taught children to read and to write—rare skills at the time.

The church was the most important building. Its columns rose to heaven. The monks gathered there seven times a day and even in the middle of the night to chant beautiful prayers, hymns, and psalms. The Mass was celebrated every day.

The library: The Bible and ancient Greek and Latin texts were very carefully housed here. This is where the monks studied. Some became scholars, whose wisdom was sought after by princes and kings. Some of them became bishops and even popes.

The fields: Peasants worked alongside the monks in the fields and chopped wood in the surrounding forests.

Byzantium
The Roman Empire in the East

In the year 324, Roman Emperor Constantine decided to build a new capital for his vast empire. He hired forty thousand builders to construct a sumptuous city in the town of Byzantium. The new city came to be called Constantinople, which in Greek means "the city of Constantine".

Byzance, center of the world

Constantine was the first Christian emperor. Thanks to him, Christians in the Roman Empire were no longer persecuted. Also, Constantine helped conflicting groups of Christians to settle their differences in meetings of bishops called councils. Throughout the empire, magnificent churches were erected. The greatest of these was the basilica of Saint Sophia, built in Constantinople by Emperor Justinian in the year 548 (basilica is a Greek word meaning "church of the king").

Beginning in the fourth century, invaders threatened the Roman Empire from all sides. The western half of the empire eventually collapsed, but Constantinople withstood each and every assault for more than a thousand years.

Byzantine art

Byzantine architecture is fabulous. The churches are topped with several domes, and the ceilings are vaulted like the heavens. Inside the walls are covered with mosaics or frescoes (paintings on fresh plaster). Eastern Christians pray before icons that depict saints or scenes from the Bible. They believe that by meditating on these images, one can grow closer to God.

The Great Schism

Greek was spoken in the Eastern Roman Empire. In the West, people spoke Latin. The peoples of East and West not only spoke different languages but thought differently too. Over the years, a rivalry grew between the bishops of the East and those of the West. In 1054, a dispute broke out over the subject of the Holy Spirit. On this and other matters, the bishops could not come to an agreement. Thus, the bishops in the East stopped recognizing the pope, the bishop of Rome, as the head of the whole Church. This split was called the Great Schism (the Greek word *schisma* means "to cut"). Rome remained the center of the Church in the West, what is now called the Roman Catholic Church. Constantinople became the center of the Orthodox churches in Greece, Eastern Europe, Russia, and the Middle East. The city went on repelling the attacks of its enemies until 1435, when it fell to the Muslim Turks.

Byzantium
Constantine moved his capital to a port between Asia and Europe, in the country now known as Turkey. It was the perfect place to become the center of the world. Today it is called Istanbul.

Saint Louis
A King Who Loved God

Louis was twelve years old when his father died in 1226. He became the king of France. His mother, Blanche of Castille, brought him up to be a powerful and respected king and especially to love God. Louis tried to rule justly and wisely. He was such a good Christian that he was named a saint of the Church.

The hospital

Louis commissioned the construction of big houses where lepers and the poor who suffered from other diseases could be treated. Apart from the infirmaries of the monasteries, these were the first hospitals.

A king who loved the poor and the sick

My name is Daniel. I live in Paris near a great big church: Notre Dame, the cathedral. They haven't finished building it yet, but it is already so beautiful! A man with a bad stoop sometimes comes to beg in front of Notre Dame. Some people throw stones at him; others throw insults: "Get out of here, you cursed leper! Go on, go away!" My father explained to me, "That man has leprosy, a terrible disease, and everyone is afraid of catching it." Yet one day, I saw King Louis reach out his hand to this leper, saying, "Get up and have lunch with me!" The king even put clean bandages on his leg.

A king who loved justice

In the orchard near King Louis' castle, there is a very tall oak tree under which the judges consider cases. On some days, Louis sits at the foot of this tree to listen. (Me too—I love to slip into the crowd and listen.) Lots of people come: "My neighbor stole from me!" "I can't feed my family; my master took my whole harvest!" Louis defends the weak. He makes sure that all people, rich and poor, are judged fairly.

A king who fought for Jesus

My father is a soldier in the army of King Louis. He is going to fight against the Muslims who do not believe that Jesus is the Son of God and do not want any more Christians to pray at his tomb in Jerusalem. Louis has already spent many years fighting against the Muslims and trying to convert them. He was made a prisoner in Egypt with his whole army. I hope this time he will win.

The Crusades

For almost two hundred years, the European nobility and their soldiers went to Jerusalem and the surrounding area to defend the religious rights of Christians visiting or living in the Holy Land, which had been under Muslim rule since the seventh century. They were ready to give their lives, like Jesus; this is why a large cross was sewn onto their clothing. They were called crusaders, and they fought in eight major campaigns called the Crusades. The crusaders failed to build lasting Christian kingdoms in these lands.

85

Saint Francis
The Poor Man of Assisi

Around the year 1200 in the town of Assisi, Italy, business was booming.

The children of the rich merchants danced and had fun.

I hear you sold fifteen yards of silk to Laura de Foligno. Is that true, Francis?

Yes, Giacoma. We'll celebrate that tomorrow at my house. There will be musicians!

When Francis was twenty, parties, jewelry, and beautiful clothes no longer amused him.

What's wrong, Francis? Are you in love?

Yes, with Lady Poverty.

In the Assisi countryside, he started to rebuild the chapel of San Damiano.

But that took money. So he sold a batch of his father's expensive fabrics without telling him.

Furious, his father took him to court to be judged by the bishop.

Francis, with what can you repay your father?

Everything that came from him

From now on, the only one I shall call Father is God, our Father who art in heaven ...

A poor man among the poor, Francis begged for his bread.

Jesus told them, "Take no money, no sandals, and only one cloak ..."

Francis traveled. He was full of joy. His new wealth was love. From the rich and poor, scholars and the uneducated, came brothers who followed him.

In 1209, the pope gave him protection, and the bishop of Assisi money.

No, Your Excellency, if we own possessions, we'll need weapons to protect them. That's how fights begin.

Clare, a young woman of Assisi, also wanted a joyful life of poverty. She too fled from her wealthy family.

Come, Clare. Francis is waiting for you at the chapel.

Clare, you have become the daughter and servant of God almighty, our heavenly Father.

Francis became known throughout the countryside. To all, he spoke about the love of God.

Brother birds, you sing so sweetly to your Creator, who dressed you in your many-colored feathers.

One day, a young brother asked him,

"Brother Francis, may I have a book of psalms?"

No, my child. If today I give you a book of psalms, tomorrow you'll want a bigger prayer book.

The day after that, you will want a throne like that of a grand lord.

The next thing you know, you'll be saying to one of your brothers, "Bring me my big prayer book!"

This is how Francis gave amusing or poetic advice: in the Fioretti ("little flowers") or in very beautiful prayers.

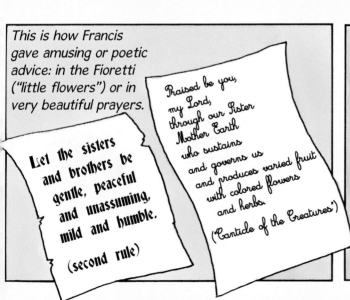

Let the sisters and brothers be gentle, peaceful and unassuming, mild and humble.

(second rule)

Praised be you, my Lord, through our Sister Mother Earth who sustains and governs us and produces varied fruit with colored flowers and herbs.

("Canticle of the Creatures")

Francis' holiness made such an impression on the brothers, they could see a halo of light around him. He was so close to Jesus, he bore the marks of the Crucifixion.

For eight hundred years now, many men and women have chosen, like Francis and Clare, to lead lives of joyful poverty for the love of God and others.

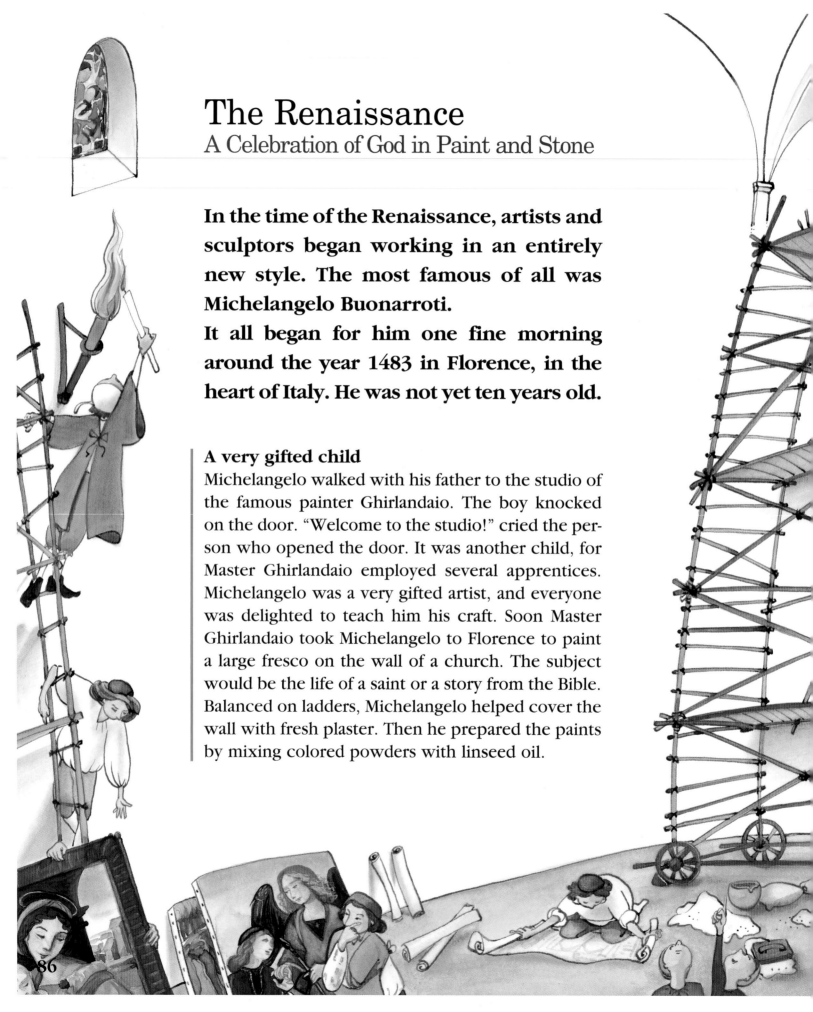

The Renaissance
A Celebration of God in Paint and Stone

In the time of the Renaissance, artists and sculptors began working in an entirely new style. The most famous of all was Michelangelo Buonarroti.

It all began for him one fine morning around the year 1483 in Florence, in the heart of Italy. He was not yet ten years old.

A very gifted child

Michelangelo walked with his father to the studio of the famous painter Ghirlandaio. The boy knocked on the door. "Welcome to the studio!" cried the person who opened the door. It was another child, for Master Ghirlandaio employed several apprentices. Michelangelo was a very gifted artist, and everyone was delighted to teach him his craft. Soon Master Ghirlandaio took Michelangelo to Florence to paint a large fresco on the wall of a church. The subject would be the life of a saint or a story from the Bible. Balanced on ladders, Michelangelo helped cover the wall with fresh plaster. Then he prepared the paints by mixing colored powders with linseed oil.

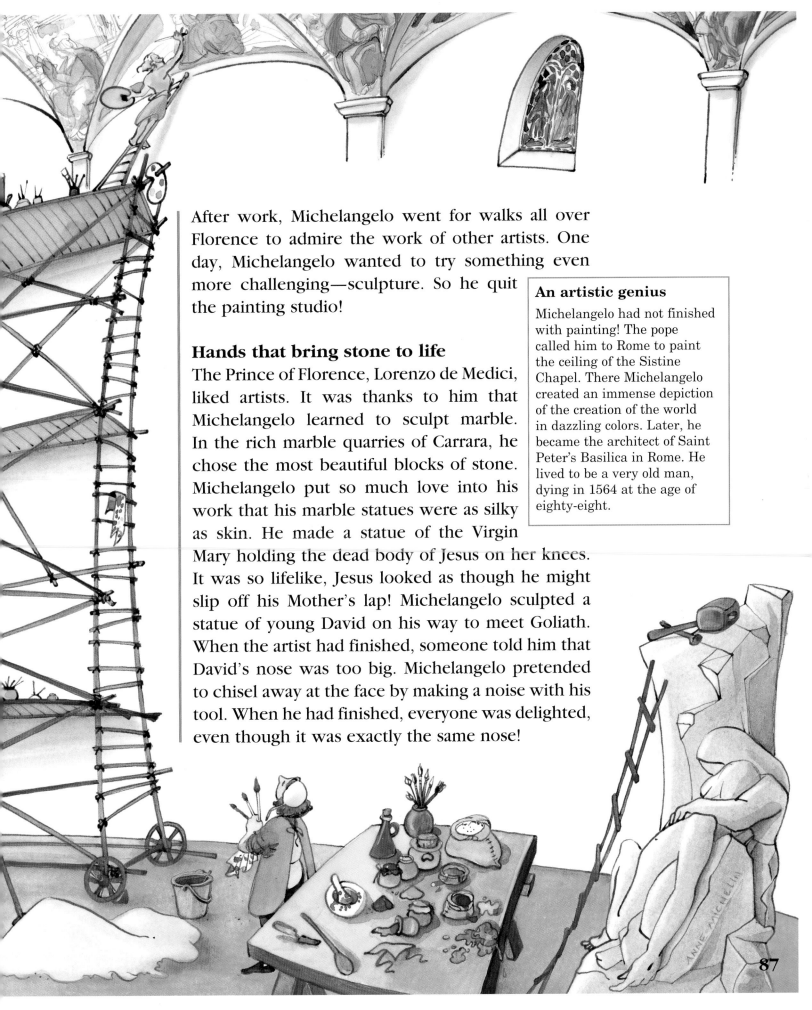

After work, Michelangelo went for walks all over Florence to admire the work of other artists. One day, Michelangelo wanted to try something even more challenging—sculpture. So he quit the painting studio!

Hands that bring stone to life

The Prince of Florence, Lorenzo de Medici, liked artists. It was thanks to him that Michelangelo learned to sculpt marble. In the rich marble quarries of Carrara, he chose the most beautiful blocks of stone. Michelangelo put so much love into his work that his marble statues were as silky as skin. He made a statue of the Virgin Mary holding the dead body of Jesus on her knees. It was so lifelike, Jesus looked as though he might slip off his Mother's lap! Michelangelo sculpted a statue of young David on his way to meet Goliath. When the artist had finished, someone told him that David's nose was too big. Michelangelo pretended to chisel away at the face by making a noise with his tool. When he had finished, everyone was delighted, even though it was exactly the same nose!

An artistic genius

Michelangelo had not finished with painting! The pope called him to Rome to paint the ceiling of the Sistine Chapel. There Michelangelo created an immense depiction of the creation of the world in dazzling colors. Later, he became the architect of Saint Peter's Basilica in Rome. He lived to be a very old man, dying in 1564 at the age of eighty-eight.

The Protestant Reformation
Christians Torn Apart

During the Renaissance, some people criticized the popes and bishops for having wealth and power. They wanted changes in the Church. Eventually the Church reformed herself, but not before many terrible conflicts had torn Christians apart.

Those who became Protestants

My name is Peter, and I live in Germany. I've been a Protestant since the age of ten. One day, merchants came to see my father in his linen shop. They told him how the monk named Martin Luther had started a revolution in the Church. Luther had rebelled against the pope and some priests who were teaching the people that they could earn their way into heaven by giving money to the Church. Luther said that you go to heaven because you believe in God and not because of your good works. He said that we should stop praying to the saints and that we should read the Bible. Luther claimed that the pope was wrong about many things and that we should not listen to him anymore. So the pope condemned

him! Some of the German princes and townsmen protested on Luther's side. The merchant said they were now called Protestants.

Germany divided

My father sided with Luther. He bought a translation of the Bible in our own language, which had become possible for people like us because of the new printing presses. Every evening, he read to us from it. My parents made friends with others who didn't want to go to Mass anymore. They met together to pray and read the Bible. All of Germany, it seemed, was choosing one side or the other.

So much hatred!

At first, everything went fine, but then conflicts began breaking out between Protestants and Catholics. On top of that, the Protestants began breaking up into different groups who could not tolerate one another. Horrible things were done by all sides—and not only in Germany. All over Europe—in England, France, Switzerland, and Holland—Christians were fighting against Christians. It was terrible! These conflicts contributed to all-out war between rival countries, such as England and Spain. Now that I'm a very old man, I pray that God will one day reunite his Church.

What happened next

After years of civil war in his country, King Henry IV of France established peace between Catholics and Protestants. In 1598, he proclaimed a law allowing Protestants to practice their faith: the Edict of Nantes. This was the first time that Catholics and Protestants were allowed to coexist as equals in the same country.

The Catholic Reformation
Great Changes and Great Saints

In the sixteenth century, many Catholics came to recognize that the Church needed to make some changes. Some men and women reformed their lives, and several became great saints who contributed to the renewal of the Catholic faith.

The Council of Trent

The Holy Roman Emperor Charles V asked the pope to convene a council of the bishops. This was very difficult to organize! Some of the bishops were in no hurry to change the way they were used to doing things. Finally, in 1545, the council was opened in Trent, Italy. The talks were long and stormy. Everyone had an opinion, and more than one bishop would speak or shout at the same time! At last, after eighteen years, important agreements were reached. Alas, reconciliation with the Protestants still had not been achieved.

Changes in the Church:

The pope and the bishops reviewed every aspect of the Church's faith and life. Here are some of the important results of the council:

- The Catholic faith was more clearly defined.
- Reading the Bible was made more important.
- The quality of religious education, especially for priests, was improved.
- Bishops were required to be the spiritual leaders of their people.

Saint Ignatius of Loyola

Ignatius of Loyola was a Spanish soldier. One day, he was wounded in battle. While he was recovering, he had a change of heart. He wanted to live and die no longer for worldly glory but for the glory of God. He gathered men to be soldiers for Christ. They became priests in the Society of Jesus, which came to be known as the Jesuits. With prayer, discipline, and learning, they heroically spread the faith to every corner of the world.

Saint Teresa of Ávila and Saint John of the Cross

Placed in a convent until she was ready to marry, Teresa gave her life to Jesus. She developed such devotion that her whole life became one immense prayer rising to God. "He hears me," she said, "and I know how to listen to him." She and Saint John of the Cross reformed Carmelite monasteries throughout Spain, turning them into powerhouses of prayer.

Saint Charles Borromeo

An Italian archbishop, Charles Borromeo was such a good man that other bishops sought to follow his example. When the plague ravaged his hometown of Milan, he aided the sick with no thought for himself. He also founded seminaries for the education of priests.

Saint Thomas More

The scholar Thomas More was a married man with children. Under King Henry VIII, he served as the chancellor of England. Ten years before the Council of Trent began, More was beheaded for refusing to declare that the king, not the pope, was the head of the Church in England. Before his death he had said, "I am the king's good servant—but God's first."

Saint Vincent de Paul and Saint Louise de Marillac

Vincent de Paul stood up to those in power, including Queen Anne of Austria, in defense of the poor, the orphans, and the galley slaves. He said, "Everywhere in France, let us open our sanctuaries to the poor and the unfortunate!" With his great friend Louise de Marillac, he founded the Sisters of Charity, an order of nuns devoted to the service of the poor.

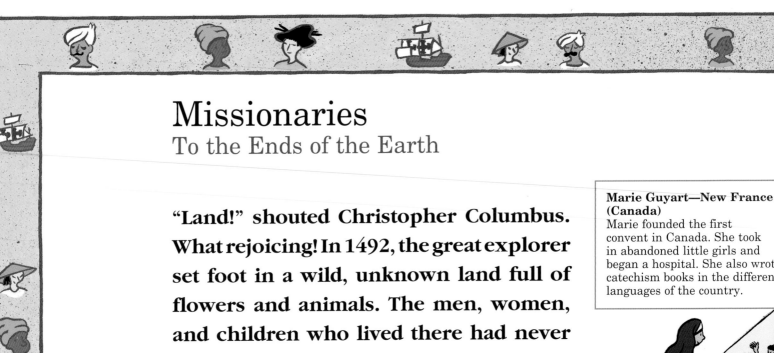

Missionaries
To the Ends of the Earth

"Land!" shouted Christopher Columbus. What rejoicing! In 1492, the great explorer set foot in a wild, unknown land full of flowers and animals. The men, women, and children who lived there had never heard about Jesus. Missionaries set off on this adventure to proclaim the good news about God's love throughout the New World. Other missionaries traveled east to Asia with the same goal.

Marie Guyart—New France (Canada)
Marie founded the first convent in Canada. She took in abandoned little girls and began a hospital. She also wrote catechism books in the different languages of the country.

Bartolomé de Las Casas—New Spain (Mexico)
Bartolomé had only one thought in mind: to become a priest and to preach to the Native Americans in New Spain. When he arrived, he saw men beating their slaves and making money by working them to death. "These are men, the same as you! Do not beat them!" he said. The Spanish landowners did not listen to him, but Father Bartolomé was determined! He spent his whole life defending the Native Americans against injustice.

The Jesuits—Latin America
There were many Jesuit missionaries in Latin America. They spoke about Jesus and brought with them all their scientific knowledge. They helped the native people organize themselves into communities so they could lead a better life.

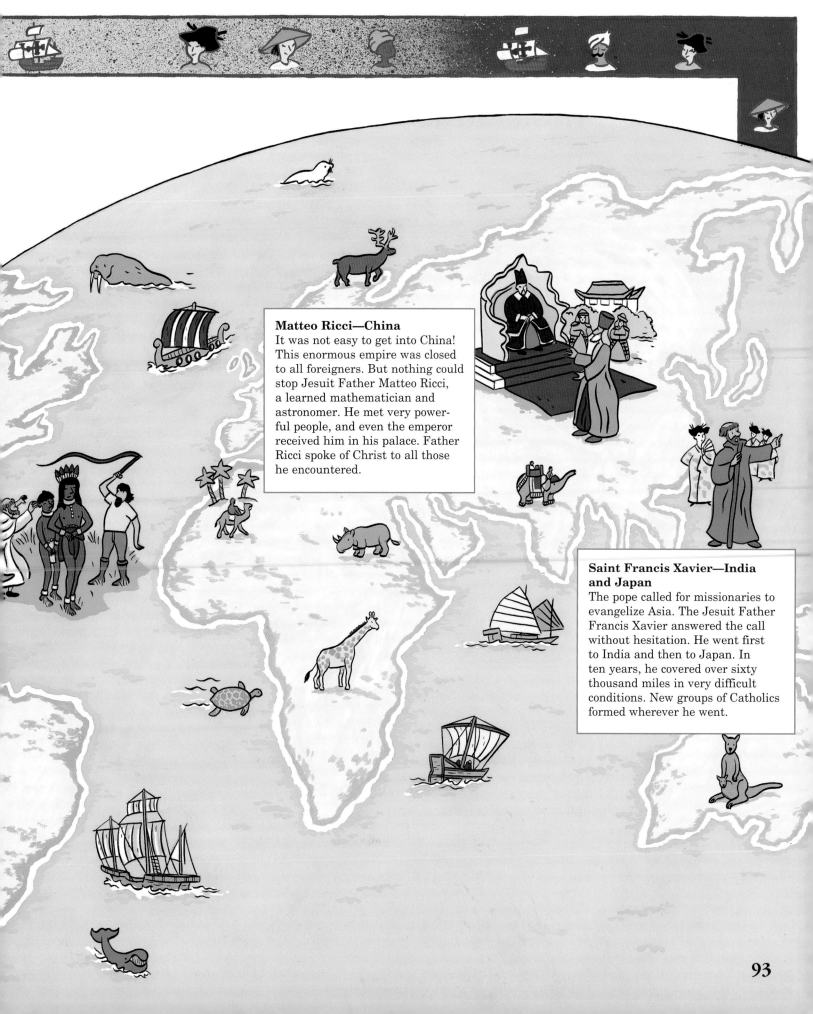

Matteo Ricci—China

It was not easy to get into China! This enormous empire was closed to all foreigners. But nothing could stop Jesuit Father Matteo Ricci, a learned mathematician and astronomer. He met very powerful people, and even the emperor received him in his palace. Father Ricci spoke of Christ to all those he encountered.

Saint Francis Xavier—India and Japan

The pope called for missionaries to evangelize Asia. The Jesuit Father Francis Xavier answered the call without hesitation. He went first to India and then to Japan. In ten years, he covered over sixty thousand miles in very difficult conditions. New groups of Catholics formed wherever he went.

Kateri Tekakwitha
The Lily of the Mohawks

During a night of high winds, huddled inside a Mohawk chief's cabin, Prairie Flower gave birth to her baby, Bright Sky. Leaning over her baby's cradle, she dreamed about what her daughter might be when she grew up.

Tekakwitha, she who goes hesitantly

Bright Sky was a happy little girl. Her father taught her to walk. Her mother, Prairie Flower, spoke to her about the God of the Christians, whom she had learned about from the priests in her old village.

Bright Sky was just four when her parents died from a terrible illness. She survived the illness but it left her almost blind. People called her Tekakwitha, "she who goes hesitantly". Fortunately, her uncle Great Wolf took care of her.

Bright Sky was a hard worker. She would draw water and prepared the animal hides. She always had a smile on her lips. But she missed her mother's prayers terribly.

The arrival of the Black Robes

One day, missionary priests in long black robes came to settle among the tribe. How courageous

they were! They had braved the cold and the Canadian forests with all their wild animals just to get there. The little girl loved to listen to them. They spoke about God as her mother had. She wanted to be baptized, but her uncle forbade it. Despite her uncle's opposition, she was finally baptized when she was twenty. Everyone made fun of her for being a Christian, and some even threw stones at her.

Kateri, the first Native American nun

Finally Great Wolf threatened, "If you go on praying to this Great Spirit, I'll kill you!" That was too much! One night, Bright Sky fled to a Catholic village. There she was at last able to pray without having to hide. One Christmas Eve, she made her First Communion. Her face shone with happiness. She met some nuns who tended the sick and took care of children. Bright Sky realized that God was calling her to become a nun. She took the name Kateri, in honor of Saint Catherine. She was the first Native American nun.

Kateri, the saint

Pope John Paul II beatified Kateri Tekakwitha in 1980, and Pope Benedict XVI canonized her in 2012. This Native American saint has become an example for all Christians.

Sister Rosalie
The Great Mission to Africa

"Go out to all the world and make disciples." In the nineteenth century, many religious took this request of Jesus very seriously. They traveled far and wide to preach the good news about God's love.

In Africa

My name is Rosalie. I came here seven years ago with three other missionary sisters to help Father Bernard. The trip here was an adventure in itself. We boarded a boat in Barcelona, Spain. Sister Bertha was sick during the whole two months of the crossing. Fortunately, I have good sea legs, but still, when there were storms, I was very frightened.

Once we had landed, we had a long way to walk. It was so hot! What a surprise when we arrived: there wasn't even a church; just an infirmary in a hut! Men and women would cross the forest to be treated by Father Bernard. They called him the great white witch doctor.

An extraordinary adventure

The village has grown now. We tend to the sick in

a little hospital, and we also take in orphans. Here they get enough to eat; we take care of them and teach them a trade. They are almost like our own children.

We get up early in the morning to pray and to go to Mass, and we take a nap after lunch when it's just too hot to work.

We speak to the children about God, who loves all men, black and white. We also tell them that the pope condemned slavery and has called for all men to respect one another.

Life here is fascinating. I feel really useful and have achieved my life's dream: to speak about Jesus to those who don't yet know him.

Missionaries in America

During the nineteenth century, many missionaries from Europe came to America. **Saint Frances Cabrini** wanted to be a missionary to China, but the pope sent her to the United States instead. She founded orphanages and hospitals in big cities such as New York and Chicago. **Saint Damien** was a missionary to the Hawaiian Islands. He volunteered to work in a leper colony that no one even dared to visit. He tirelessly cared for those suffering from leprosy, until he died of the dreaded disease himself. This period saw American-born missionaries too. **Saint Katherine Drexel** was from a wealthy Philadelphia family. She dedicated herself and her inheritance to serving and educating poor Native Americans and black Americans.

Lourdes
The Blessed Virgin Mary and Saint Bernadette

Bernadette lived in Lourdes, a little town in the south of France, in the 1800s. Her father was a miller until he lost his job, and the family became very poor. They even had to sell their house! Bernadette worked hard to help her parents. She did not go to school very often, but she loved to pray. One day, the Blessed Virgin Mary appeared to her.

Bernadette fell to her knees

Bernadette was fourteen. She went with her sister Toinette and a girlfriend to gather wood at the grotto of Massabielle. Suddenly she fell to her knees, motionless, as if she had been turned to stone.

"What did you see?" asked Toinette.

"In the hole in the rock, I saw a very beautiful lady in white, with a blue sash and a yellow rose at each foot. She took her rosary beads and made the Sign of the Cross."

"You're just saying that to scare us!"

In Lourdes, this apparition was all anyone could talk about. What a commotion! "I wish so much that I could see the lovely lady in white again", thought Bernadette.

I am the Immaculate Conception

She returned to the foot of the rock to pray. At first, the lady smiled but did not say anything. Then one day she asked Bernadette, "Would you be kind enough to come here for the next fifteen days?" Bernadette was astonished that the lady had spoken to her as if she were someone important! The parish priest had told Bernadette to ask the lady for her name. "I am the Immaculate Conception", she said. Bernadette did not understand, but she ran to the priest and repeated to him exactly what the lady had said. The priest was astounded: "The name Immaculate Conception means that from her mother's womb, Mary was untouched by sin. This purity was a special gift from God so that she could be the Mother of Jesus."

Every day, more and more people came to the grotto of Massabielle. Water had started flowing from a spring that Bernadette had unearthed with her bare hands, and sick people were being healed there. Some of these cures have been declared miraculous because there is no scientific explanation for them.

A pilgrimage site

People still visit Lourdes. At nightfall, there is a procession in front of the grotto. People carry large candles as children sing songs to the Blessed Virgin Mary. Crowds of pilgrims come from all over the world. Some hope to be cured by bathing in the healing water.

Bernadette, the nun

After the appearances of the Blessed Virgin Mary, Bernadette became a simple nun in Nevers, far from Lourdes. She suffered much from illness and died in 1879 while still a young woman. Her greatest joy was in knowing that through her the Blessed Virgin Mary had strengthened the faith of many people. She was canonized in 1933.

Science and Technology
New Challenges to the Faith

Many people today do not believe in Jesus Christ and think that we can do without God. How did that happen?

Scientific discoveries

Three hundred years ago, almost everyone in the Western world believed in Jesus Christ. There were differences between them, according to whether they were Catholic, Protestant, or Orthodox. They tried to explain the world using the knowledge of their times. If they did not understand something, they said it was a mystery. Beginning in the 1700s, scientists began making big discoveries. They showed that some of the mysteries of the universe could be explained by science. Nothing was the same again!

Modern thinkers

Some thinkers declared that God existed, but that people did not need Jesus Christ and his Church. For some, God was everywhere, in nature. Others thought that God made the world work, like a master clockmaker, or even that he was the great architect who designed the universe. But they did not

believe that God was the loving Father who took a personal interest in mankind. Still others thought that God was made up, like a fairy tale, and that it was pointless to believe in him.

Christians and scientists reconciled

Christians do not believe that scientific discoveries are enough to bring happiness on earth, but they know that scientists have a lot of fascinating things to teach us about the world that God created. For their part, scientists know that they cannot explain the greatest mysteries: Why was I born? What is love? Is there life after death? What must I do to be happy? Many people, whether they are Christian or not, still ask themselves these questions today. But Catholic Christians look for answers with the help of Jesus and his Church.

Free to believe!

In the twentieth century, some dictators persecuted Christians in the name of their dream of a perfect society, which they thought could only come about without God and religion. But there are also many good, peaceful people who do not believe in God. They simply think that God does not exist, and they are free to do so.

Maximilian Kolbe
A Saint for the Modern World

Around 1904, in the Polish village of Pabiance, at a weaver's shop.

Marianna, Raymond worries me. He's never here to help me.

Be patient, Jules. He's only ten. I must tell you, the other day I found him praying in front of the icon again.

Raymond, you're crying?

Mommy, I saw the Blessed Virgin Mary. She showed me two wreaths of flowers, one white and one red.

The white one meant I would be pure, and the red one that I would be a martyr. I told her I wanted them both.

In 1910, Poland was under Russian domination.

I'd like to be a soldier to serve my country like a knight, or maybe a monk to serve Mary, the Queen of Poland.

In 1911, Raymond became a Franciscan brother and took the name Maximilian.

Now I know that I will be a knight of our Lady.

He was sent to Rome to study. In 1917, he organized his friends into a group called the Militia Immaculata.*

We will fight evil with weapons that don't kill.

* Immaculata refers to the Immaculate Conception, one of the names for Mary, the Mother of Jesus.

These weapons were words, books and newspapers. Maximilian created a convent publishing house: Niepokalanow, which means "city of the Immaculata".

We're poor, but to serve God we must use the most modern machines.

Niepokalanow isn't just offices, machines, or magazines. It's each one of us. Every second of our whole lives belongs to Mary.

German soldiers invaded Poland in September 1939.

You're sheltering Jews in this convent!

Deported to the Auschwitz concentration camp, Maximilian never stopped bringing support to his companions in suffering.

Entrust your sorrow to Mary. She is the mother of those who suffer.

On August 2, 1941, a prisoner made an escape. After a whole day of standing at attention in the rain,

ten men were chosen at random to be condemned to death by starvation.

You! You! You!

Have mercy. I'm a married man; I have children!

I am a Catholic priest, and I wish to take his place.

He supported his companions to the end in the bunker of death.

... Holy Mary, Mother of God, pray for us, now and at the hour of our death.

Christians for Peace
A Difficult Challenge

"Blessed are the peacemakers", said Jesus. Here are a few men and women who put these words of his into practice.

"Black people didn't have the same rights as white people. I tried to move people to change things, through peace and nonviolence."

Rev. Martin Luther King — Nobel Peace Laureate — United States

"Indians are not recognized as full citizens. I battle for the recognition of their rights."

Rigoberta Menchu — Nobel Peace Laureate — Latin America

In Northern Ireland, Catholics and Protestants were at war. Suzan Sellers is a Catholic, and Mia Banks is a Protestant. "We decided to become activists for peace together instead of fighting each other."

Suzan Sellers and Mia Banks — Ireland

"I supported the Polish people in their fight to be free to be Christians and to choose their political leaders."

Fr. Jerzy Popiełuszko — Poland

"To work for peace is to give every man bread and a roof over his head. With my companions in the Emmaus Community, we welcome the homeless."

Abbé Pierre — France

"During the last war, Europeans killed each other.
Now let us try to unite. Let's build Europe!"

Robert Schuman — Europe

"Our country was invaded. I am trying to win back
our independence without violence."

Bishop Carlos Belo and José Ramos-Horta— Nobel Peace Laureate — Asia

"My country of Rwanda was torn apart by hate.
The only way to peace is through forgiveness."

Immaculée Ilibagiza—Ghandi Peace Award—Africa

Mother Teresa
The Joy of Giving

"Let no one ever come to us without leaving better and happier."

"Let us always have a smile on our lips for every child we assist."

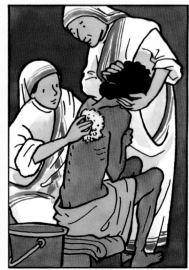

A few days later—

Why are you doing this for me?

Because I love you. Because God loves you.

Say that again, because that was the first time in my life I've heard those words.

"Heal, feed, love, so that no one may die alone, hopeless, unloved."

Some in India are so poor that children are abandoned in the streets in garbage pails.

Former students of Mother Teresa became the first sisters of the Missionaries of Charity.

There ... massage it gently ... yes ... like that.

Today thousands of men and women are Missionaries of Charity.

For the love of Jesus, they have opened homes for children, the sick, and the dying all over the world.

Mother Teresa traveled the world, founding homes for the poorest of the poor.

The Missionaries of Charity take strength from praying together three times a day.

The fruit of silence is prayer,

The fruit of prayer is faith,

The fruit of faith is love,

The fruit of love is service,

The fruit of service is peace.

A Trip to the Vatican
The Country of the Pope

With a government and a secretary of state, the head of the Catholic Church, the pope, is in charge of a tiny country called the Vatican. It has a post office, a train station, a radio station and a newspaper, museums, and of course, the immense Saint Peter's Basilica. The Vatican is built on a hill in Rome.

The heliport
The pope travels a lot and is often pressed for time. To travel faster, he uses a helicopter.

Saint Peter's Basilica
Built over the tomb of Saint Peter, this enormous church is over three hundred years old. It is topped with a famous dome that can be seen from far away. At the bronze doors, you will see Swiss Guards dressed in their curious striped uniforms.

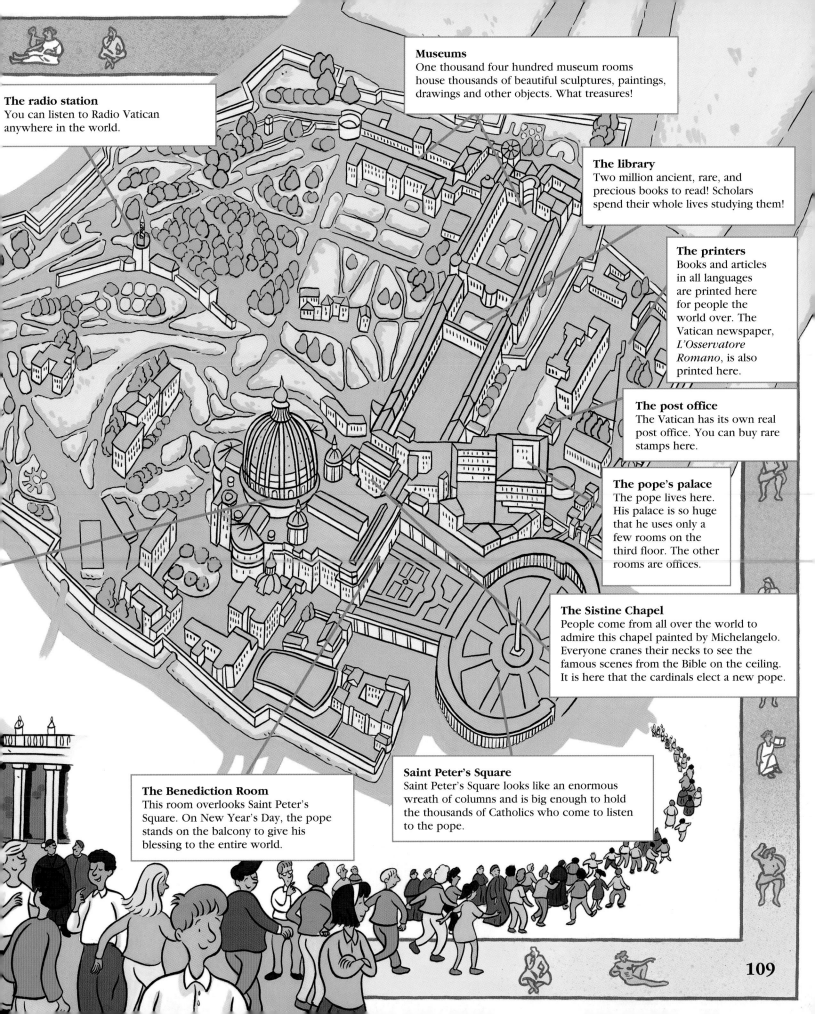

Museums
One thousand four hundred museum rooms house thousands of beautiful sculptures, paintings, drawings and other objects. What treasures!

The radio station
You can listen to Radio Vatican anywhere in the world.

The library
Two million ancient, rare, and precious books to read! Scholars spend their whole lives studying them!

The printers
Books and articles in all languages are printed here for people the world over. The Vatican newspaper, *L'Osservatore Romano*, is also printed here.

The post office
The Vatican has its own real post office. You can buy rare stamps here.

The pope's palace
The pope lives here. His palace is so huge that he uses only a few rooms on the third floor. The other rooms are offices.

The Sistine Chapel
People come from all over the world to admire this chapel painted by Michelangelo. Everyone cranes their necks to see the famous scenes from the Bible on the ceiling. It is here that the cardinals elect a new pope.

The Benediction Room
This room overlooks Saint Peter's Square. On New Year's Day, the pope stands on the balcony to give his blessing to the entire world.

Saint Peter's Square
Saint Peter's Square looks like an enormous wreath of columns and is big enough to hold the thousands of Catholics who come to listen to the pope.

The Pope
The Leader of All Catholics

The pope is the head of the Catholic Church. Along with all the bishops, he is responsible for his brothers and sisters in the faith all over the world.

The word *pope* means "father"

Jesus entrusted the Church to Peter the apostle. Since then, every pope carries on this mission of leading the Church as Peter did. Like a father, the pope does everything he can to keep the family of faith strong and united. He guides all Catholics as they follow Jesus.

Down to work!

The pope works hard. He listens to people who come from all over the world to speak to him. He chooses new bishops and cardinals, and he meets with them regularly to give them guidance and support. He writes letters of advice for the whole Church. He prays very often that he might always do the will of God.

The pope is not on his own

The pope is the bishop of Rome, and he leads the Church with the help of the other bishops—of which there are more than four thousand throughout the world. All the bishops together carry on the work of the apostles. Each bishop is responsible for

the Catholics in his area, called a diocese. With his priests, he helps his flock stay close to Jesus.

The Church reflects together
Everywhere in the world, Catholics meet to make decisions about their life together—in small parish groups or in large conferences that include the priests and the bishops of their dioceses. In the Church, no one is left out!

The cardinals choose the pope
When a pope dies, a new pope must be elected. The cardinals gather in Rome at the Vatican. They lock themselves in the Sistine Chapel for several days to pray and to reflect. They do not even leave to eat or to sleep! They stay together until they all agree on a new pope. When the pope is chosen, all the ballot papers are burned. A plume of smoke rises into the sky from the chimney: that is the signal that a decision has been made! The new pope greets the crowds waiting outside in Saint Peter's Square.

Three famous popes
In 1962, Pope John XXIII gathered two thousand bishops from all over the world for the Second Vatican Council. This giant meeting gave rise to big changes in the Church and in the lives of Catholics. After the death of Pope John XXIII, Pope Paul VI carried on this work. John Paul II was the first Polish pope. He went on several world tours to meet Catholics everywhere.

111

The Parish
Catholic Life Together

The parish welcomes everyone.

The Catholics in one neighborhood or town make up a parish.

The priest is responsible for his parish.

In the parish, we learn about our faith.

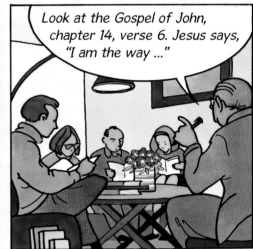

In the parish, we pray.

At the baptism of new Catholics.

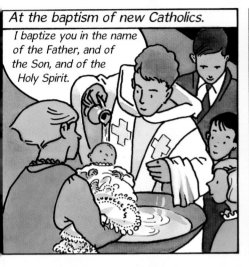

I baptize you in the name of the Father, and of the Son, and of the Holy Spirit.

At weddings

I, Emily, take you, Ryan, to be my wedded husband.

In confession

Yours sins are forgiven, in the name of the Father ...

In the parish, we organize.

We won't be able to get everything done this year.

Then it's best to start with the roof.

Here are some flowers from my garden.

Just what we need for tomorrow. These have already wilted.

We won't have any song sheets.

Yes, we will. I'll type them on my computer.

In the parish, we help others.

I haven't seen Mrs. Brown for two days.

I'll drop in to see how she is.

These two suits are too small now, but they're not worn out.

I know who could use them.

Christians in this African country would like to build a school.

The Church
The House of God for Christians

You can easily spot a church. It is a big building, often with a tower or two and a cross. Christians gather here to pray and to listen to the Word of God. Come on in; the tour of this Catholic church is about to begin!

There are **statues of saints** in niches along the side walls. Each saint has his own story. The saints are with God in heaven. We can ask them to pray for us, and sometimes we can light candles in front of their statues. May our hearts burn with the love of God as theirs did!

At this basin of water the priest baptizes children and adults. It is called **the baptismal font**.

What are these big pipes for? To make music! They are what give this instrument, **the organ**, all its power.

At the church entrance, there is a small basin of water: this is **the holy water font**. People dip their fingers into the water and bless themselves, as a reminder of their baptism.

114

On Sundays, **the church bells** ring out to let Catholics know it is time for Mass.

The tabernacle: Here is the most sacred place in the whole Church. Here the hosts that have become the Body of Christ at Mass are kept. A little red lamp shines day and night as the sign of Jesus' presence.

The crucifix: There is the cross with an image of Jesus upon it, reminding us that he loved us so much that he gave up his life for us.

...hat is that wooden ...or behind the altar? ...leads to a small room ...here the priests get ...ady for Mass. It is **the ...cristy**. The vestments, ...e books and the ...ndles are kept here.

The altar is a large wooden or stone table. It is covered with a cloth. The priest places the bread and wine on it. There he offers them to God, who returns them to us changed into his very life.

115

Following the Risen Christ
For Two Thousand Years

For two thousand years, Christians have followed the risen Christ. They have lived and proclaimed the good news of his Resurrection throughout the ages to every corner of the earth.

1. Saint Blandina
"Blessed are you when they persecute you because of my name."

2. Monastic life
"When you pray, shut the door and pray to your Father in secret."

3. Saint Francis
"Go, sell what you possess and give to the poor; and come, follow me."

4.The Renaissance
"All that you do, do for the glory of God."

5. Mission to the New World
"Proclaim the good news to all of creation."

6. Saint Bernadette
"I thank you, Father, that you have kept these things hidden from the wise and understanding and revealed them to children."

7. Mission to Africa
"Go and make disciples of all nations, baptizing them in the name of the Father and of the Son and of the Holy Spirit."

8. Martin Luther King
"Blessed are the peacemakers, for they will be called children of God."

9. Mother Teresa
"As you did it to one of the least of these my brethren, you did it to me."

10. The pope
"You are Peter, and upon this rock I will build my Church."

11. The Mass
"I am with you always, to the end of the age."

3

The Catholic Faith

The Beliefs and Sacraments

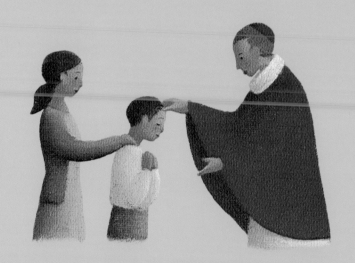

The Big Questions

Faith Does Not Stop Us from Asking Why

There are easy little questions that we can answer right away, without much thinking. There are more difficult questions that we have to think about for a while. And then there are big questions that no one can fully answer.

So many questions!

You cannot sleep. So many questions are running around in your head. Why are there so many wars? Why do people hurt each other? You toss and turn. Why are there earthquakes that kill innocent people? Why are some children born handicapped? It seems so unfair! You get out of bed to go ask your parents, and they tell you, "These are difficult questions, and it is late at night. Let's talk about them in the morning." When you still cannot sleep, you start asking yourself even more questions: Where was I before I was born? Why am I here? Why do people die?

Everyone wonders

Lots of people ask these big questions: not only you, but your parents and your friends too. Scientists, philosophers and theologians, presidents, and even popes wonder about the same things! Before you

were born, people were asking these questions; people all over the world are asking them now. Although people might not have all the answers, they go on living and loving. Finally, you fall asleep, wake up in the morning, and go on playing and studying and loving as before.

The search must go on

Keep on doing these things, but go on asking questions too. Do not be afraid. Do not get discouraged. As you learn more, you will understand more, even if some questions will never be completely answered here and now.

You will find that even without all the answers, you can still believe in God and trust in him. Faith does not stop us from asking big questions, nor does asking them stop us from having faith. Indeed, our desire to know, our longing for the truth, leads us to God, who alone knows everything.

Lights twinkling in the darkness

Artists have created works of art in their search for the truth. They have painted pictures, written poems, and composed music. Each of these works sheds its own little light on the big questions.

121

To Believe
What Does That Mean?

In everyday life, we believe lots of things and lots of people. Grown-ups believe what journalists say on television. Children believe their schoolteachers. Sick people believe their doctors. Why do we believe without knowing, without seeing, without touching? And to believe in God? Is that the same thing?

To believe without seeing

When you read in your geography book, "The earth is round", you do not disagree with your book even though the earth seems flat to you. You do not set off on a world tour to see for yourself whether the earth is round. Great scientists have studied the subject. Everyone believes that what they say is true. It is the same with lots of very simple things.

If you love, you believe!

If your godfather who lives in New York City phones you in Los Angeles and says, "It's snowing here today", you have no proof that what he says is true. Maybe you find it a bit funny because, at the same moment, it is sunny where you are! But since

you know that your godfather loves you, you trust him: you believe him even without seeing the snow in New York.

If you have trust, you believe

It is the same thing with Christian faith. To believe in God, in Jesus, is to have trust in him because you know that he loves you. This trust comes from the heart. It does not contradict what our minds know to be true, but it is not based on scientific proofs. Of course, we try to understand our faith with our minds; but our belief in God is based on his love for us, which we know through our experience and the experience of others.

Consider this: When you were a baby, your dad tossed you in the air and caught you in his arms. It made you burst out with laughter. You were not at all scared. You trusted in his strength. To believe in God is a little like that. You are a little child in God's arms; you know that he loves you; you understand that you can count on him. You believe in him. You know that he will never let you down.

123

There Are Many Religions
Men and Women in Search of God

For millennia, people everywhere have asked the same questions: Why are we alive? Why do people suffer? How can I be happy? What happens after we die? Many people believe in God, but not everyone understands him in the same way or calls him by the same name. There are many religions, and they share much in common; but there are important differences between them too.

Christianity

Christians believe in one God in three persons: the Father, the Son, and the Holy Spirit. The one true God created everything and is the Father of everyone. He revealed himself in a special way to the Jews. God the Son came to earth in the form of a man, Jesus Christ. Jesus died on the Cross and rose from the dead to save all mankind. The love of the Father and the Son is the Holy Spirit, who unites Christians with God and with one another.

Judaism

Jews believe there is one God, who created everything and chose them to be his people. God freed them from slavery and gave them his laws, including the Ten Commandments. Through his prophets, God promised to send his people the Messiah, who would bring salvation to the whole world. Jesus, his Mother Mary, the apostles, and many disciples were Jews. They believed that Jesus was the promised Messiah.

Hinduism

For Hindus, there is only one God, but he takes many forms and names, such as Vishnu and Shiva. Hindus believe that after a person dies, he is born again in a different body and that after living many good lives, he can reach the perfect peace of Nirvana. Hindus wash away their sins in the sacred river of India, the Ganges.

Islam

The word *Islam* means "submission to God". Muslims believe in one God, whom they call Allah. They believe that Allah told their prophet Muhammad how people must live in order to enter paradise. These teachings are in the Qur'an. The Qur'an retells some stories from the Bible, but it says that Jesus did not die on the Cross and rise from the dead, that he was only a prophet and not the Son of God.

Buddhism

This religion was inspired by the life of Siddhartha Gautama, a Hindu. Siddhartha believed that suffering is caused by the desires in our hearts. He taught that we could end suffering through meditation and self-discipline that leads to right thinking and right acting. His friends called him Buddha, which means "enlightened".

Billions of Christians
All Followers of Jesus

Christianity is the largest religion in the world. A third of the world's population, more than two billion people, is Christian. Half of these Christians are Catholics, making the Catholic Church the largest Christian group worldwide. The other half are either Orthodox or Protestant.

In **the United States**, almost 80 percent of the population is Christian. While one-fourth of American Christians are Catholic, most belong to various Protestant churches or even to no church at all. Many are also Orthodox. The great advocate of African-American civil rights, Martin Luther King, was a Protestant minister.

The majority of the world's Catholics live in **Latin America**. The archbishop of San Salvador, Oscar Romero, died in defense of the poor in 1980.

In **Germany and Scandinavia**, there are many Lutherans, named after their founder, Martin Luther.

The Anglican Church was started when an English king declared himself, instead of the pope, to be the head of Christians in **England**. Anglicans live in English-speaking countries everywhere, and their worldwide leader is the archbishop of Canterbury. Anglicans in America are called Episcopalians.

The Reformed churches were begun in **Geneva, Switzerland**, by John Calvin and have spread throughout the world. Other kinds of Protestants as well as Catholics also live in Switzerland.

In **Russia**, almost all Christians are Orthodox.

Rome is the capital city of Catholics: It was here that Peter the apostle died. His successor is the pope, who lives in the Vatican.

Istanbul, formerly Constantinople, is the home of Orthodox Christianity. There are many Orthodox Christians throughout the world, particularly in Greece, Russia, and Eastern Europe. They have a deep devotion to Mary, the Mother of God, and to the saints. They chant their prayers in beautiful ancient liturgies.

Christians are a minority in **Calcutta, India**, where most people are Hindu. This is where Mother Teresa and her nuns began sheltering the dying and caring for them with love.

In **South Africa**, the Anglican archbishop of Cape Town, Desmond Tutu, is a famous champion of peace and reconciliation between black people and white people. Christianity is growing rapidly throughout Africa.

Christians are a minority in **Asia**, except in the Philippines, where most people are Catholic. Protestants and Catholics combined make up a third of the population of South Korea. In China, where religion is harshly persecuted by the government, there are millions of Christians, both Protestant and Catholic, but their exact number is unknown.

An Invitation
God Offers His Friendship to All

On the first morning in his new school, Ben was all alone. He did not know anyone, and he watched the others playing. One child approached him and said, "Hi, my name is Paul. What's yours? Would you like to play with me?" They talked and became friends. Catholics believe that God behaves in the same way. He offers his friendship to everyone.

A God who comes to meet us

Just as Paul went to meet Ben, God comes to meet us. He makes the first step.

Just as Paul spoke to Ben, God speaks to us. God invites us to be his friend. We are free to accept or refuse this invitation. Why does God come to meet us? It is because he loves us, and he knows we can be happy only if we accept and return his love.

A God who loves forever

God is eternal and infinite. Likewise his love is so immense that it is without end and without limits. That is the reason it can include everyone.

A God who is all-powerful

God is so powerful that he can remove all the barriers between us and him, even our sins. When we accept his invitation to be his friend, nothing can stand in our way.

A God who speaks to us

God is interested in each one of us. Of course, we do not see God with our eyes. We cannot touch him with our hands. But God is still someone you can really meet. When we are quiet, God lets us know he is there. He speaks to us, and we can respond to him with trust.

129

God the Father
The Model for Fatherhood

It is difficult to imagine what God is like. Is he like a judge who gives out punishments? A doting grandpa who lets us do anything we want? A very powerful king who forces us to do his will? A magician who tries to impress and entertain us with tricks? No! God is not like any of these. God is the best of fathers.

Giver of everything good

God is the giver of life. That makes him the father of everyone: kids, grown-ups, the poor, even people we think are nasty. He is also the source of all the good things we depend on every day: the air we breathe, the water we drink, and the food we eat. No one can say, "God doesn't love me!" God gives life and love to all.

Closer than any human father

God is everywhere, even in the depths of our hearts. So he is closer to us than any human father could ever be. Day or night, at home or at school, in happiness or sadness, God is with us. He comforts us when we are sad, listens when we tell him the secrets of our hearts, and rejoices when we do something good. God never forgets about us; he never lets us down.

Both gentle and challenging

God takes us gently but firmly in his arms. He carries us clasped tenderly to his heart. He steadies us as we learn difficult things. He lifts us up when we fall. He looks for us when we stray onto the wrong track. God never abandons us. He loves us so much that he always forgives us when we are sorry.

God also challenges us. He wants his children to grow, to become strong in doing good so that they can be happy. From time to time, he seems strict, but he is always just. He is the wise father who teaches his children the difference between right and wrong. Listening to God and obeying him is not blindly following empty rules, but letting him love us and loving him more and more in return.

Jesus leads us to the Father

Jesus teaches us, and shows us, the power of God's love. In everything Jesus said and did, we see that God's love is the most powerful thing there is, greater even than sin and death.

God the Son
The Savior of His Brothers and Sisters

We love our dad, our mom, our brothers, our sisters, and our friends; that is natural. But those who are very different from us—how can we love them?

A message of love

Jesus, the Son of God, came to live on earth to save all men. He showed us that he was one with the Father by his miracles—curing the sick, walking on water, calming a storm, even raising the dead to life. The greatest thing Jesus did was to die for our sins and then rise from the dead, proving in the greatest way possible God's love for us. Jesus said: "Love one another, as I have loved you." He asks us to imitate him by loving others.

Love no matter what!

Everyone gets annoyed with others sometimes. Maybe someone at school teases you. Maybe an older neighbor or relative constantly complains. Jesus tells us not to get angry at others but to try to understand them and to live with them in peace. How do we do that?

Look in a new light

Thanks to Jesus, all men and women are brothers and sisters, children of the same God. When we look at others in this light, we see that loving others, even those we do not like that much, is possible.

Jesus asks us to see others as made by God, in his image, and loved by him, rather than noticing only their faults. God gives everyone something of himself. When we look for that in others and admire it, we can give thanks and praise to God for all the wonderful people he has made! Jesus even went so far as to say, "Love your enemies; pray for those who harm you." That is a big task. But to help Christians do this, Jesus sent the Holy Spirit.

Saint Thérèse of Lisieux

Thérèse lived in a convent, and one of the other nuns there really got on her nerves. Instead of being unpleasant to her, Thérèse decided to love her even more than all the others. Whenever she met her, she said a prayer for her. In this way, Thérèse grew in her ability to love.

God the Holy Spirit
The Bond of Love

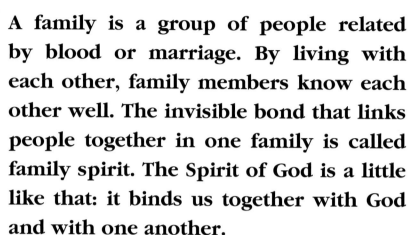

A family is a group of people related by blood or marriage. By living with each other, family members know each other well. The invisible bond that links people together in one family is called family spirit. The Spirit of God is a little like that: it binds us together with God and with one another.

The Spirit of God is love

God is not alone. Within himself, he is a family. There is only one God, but his oneness is made up of three persons: the Father, the Son, and the Holy Spirit. The Father gives the Son, Jesus, to mankind. Jesus receives everything from the Father and gives everything back to him in return by doing his will. And who is the Spirit? The Spirit is the love shared by the Father and the Son, the bond that unites them. God wants us to share in this communion of love by receiving the Holy Spirit.

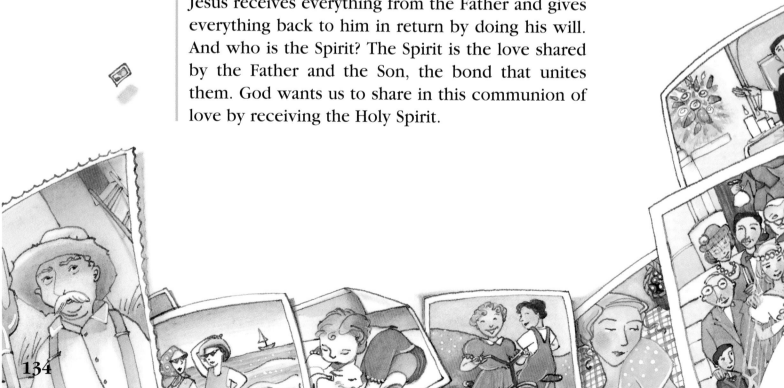

The great family of Christians

The Holy Spirit is truly present today in the lives of Christians. Through the Spirit we recognize that Jesus is the Son of God. Through the Spirit we call God our Father. The Spirit knits us together as one family and gives us the ability to love and forgive one another. Sadly, Christians are divided into many groups that do not agree about how they are to live out their faith in Christ. Jesus prayed that his followers would be one in the Spirit as he and the Father are one. We can pray and work for this unity too!

Where there is love, there is the Spirit of God

When a man and a woman get married, they remain two separate people. And yet between this man and this woman there is something quite new, which did not exist before they met. There is a very strong bond that unites them. This bond is all the love they have for each other. This love is so strong that the two spouses live in communion with each other and become one.

135

The Catholic Church
Catholic Christians

To be a Catholic Christian does not mean to believe in God off in your own little corner! Catholics are part of the big Christian family throughout the world called the Catholic Church. The word *catholic* means "universal".

Jesus gathers his Church

Jesus himself founded the Church. He gathered his friends, the disciples, around him and taught them how to live together. To his apostles he gave authority to guide and serve his followers, and to Peter he gave special responsibility to take care of the other apostles. Those Christians all over the world who follow Peter's successor, the pope, are part of the Catholic Church. Those Christians who do not accept the leadership of the pope are members of other churches.

Here are some images from the New Testament that help us understand what the Catholic Church is:

The Church is a people

The Church is a people walking toward God, with Jesus leading the way. Jesus shows us the path we should take, and we trust and follow him without

fear. We can think of these people as being on a pilgrimage, journeying together through this life on their way to heaven.

The Church is a body
The Church is the body of Christ. Christ is the head of his body, and each baptized person is a member of it. All the members are joined together and do their special part for the good of the whole body.

The Church is a house
Believers are like the living stones that form the house of God. The Holy Spirit unites them, like mortar that holds the stones together, and God dwells among them within the house.

The Church is a field
The Church is the field of God. Those who believe in Christ are the wheat that he has sown. Just as plants need care and the sun and the rain to make them grow and bear fruit, the faithful, too, need care and life from God in order to become mature Christians.

The words *church* and *Church*

The word *church* with a small c is the place where Catholics or other Christians gather to worship God. This church is a building that you can see with your eyes; you can touch its walls and hear the sound of its bells. The word *Church* with a capital C means the Catholic Church throughout the world.

The Credo

The Profession of Faith

Every Sunday at Mass, Catholics listen to the Word of God. Then they recite together a profession of faith in God, the Father, Son, and Holy Spirit. It is the creed, which comes from the Latin word *credo*, meaning "I believe". The following version is the Apostles' Creed, which is also prayed at the beginning of the Rosary.

I believe in God, the Father almighty,
Creator of heaven and earth,

and in Jesus Christ, his only Son,
our Lord,
who was conceived by the Holy Spirit,
born of the Virgin Mary,
suffered under Pontius Pilate,
was crucified, died, and was buried;
he descended into hell;
on the third day he rose again from the dead;
he ascended into heaven
and is seated at the right hand of God,
the Father almighty;
from there he will come to judge
the living and the dead.

I believe in the Holy Spirit,
the holy catholic Church,
the communion of saints,
the forgiveness of sins,
the resurrection of the body,
and life everlasting.

Amen.

God Does Not Like Death
He Gives Life Everlasting

Even if you are a child, you already know that death is sad. You do not want to die. You are afraid that those you love might die. God does not like death either. He wants to share his life with us forever.

The gift of life forever

God gives life. What joy there is when a baby comes into the world! God never wishes the death of anyone. He does not want men to be sad or afraid. That is why Jesus offers everlasting life to everyone. When we accept this gift from Jesus, we hope that after we die we will rise to a new life of perfect happiness that will last forever.

The faithful departed

Even though Christians are sad to see loved ones die and are unhappy to be separated from them, they hope that their departed loved ones will live with God for eternity.

Prayers for the dead

Catholics pray for those who have died, that God will welcome them into the company of his saints in heaven. The saints pray for us on earth that we will stay close to Jesus throughout our lives and accept his gift of eternal life.

Evil and Sin
What Distances Us from God

Evil, sin: perhaps these words scare you a little. But they do not just concern grown-ups. Children too are capable of sin.

Doing wrong

Your brother was given candy for his birthday. You know the candy is not yours, but you have a sweet tooth. You know you should not eat it; that would make your brother so unhappy! Yet that is just what you do. Knowing an action is wrong and choosing to do it anyway is committing a sin. A sin is not a silly mistake; it is a freely chosen act. On the playground, you knock a friend down without meaning to. That is not a sin; it is just an accident. You help your friend up, and it is all over. But when you purposely trip someone who annoys you, you intend to hurt him even though you know that hurting him is wrong. That is a sin. Sin saddens God because it separates us from him and makes us unhappy.

Love is stronger than evil

Jesus was put to death even though he was completely innocent and never did any wrong. Out of love for mankind, Jesus willingly took upon himself the sins of men. He gave himself up to God the Father by dying on the Cross. Through his Resurrection, Jesus saved all men of all times and places from sin and death. Thus, the infinite love of God is stronger than evil.

Have trust

Everyone sins, but God is always ready to forgive anyone who asks. God never withdraws his faith in us. He gives us the freedom to do the right thing, even knowing that sometimes we will choose to do the wrong thing. God understands us and loves us completely. That is why we can turn to him in trust when we have sinned: we know God wants to give us his mercy and the strength we need to behave better each day.

Be careful not to feel responsible for other people's decisions. Misfortunes can happen to us that are not our fault, such as the divorce of one's parents. If bad things that are not our fault happen to us or to our families, we can pray and trust that God will bring good out of those bad things.

Joseph and his brothers

Joseph had many brothers, and they were so jealous of him that they sold him to slave traders. Joseph was taken to Egypt, where he became an important government official. During a famine, Joseph's brothers went to Egypt to buy grain. When they recognized Joseph, they begged for his mercy. Joseph forgave them, saying, "Be at peace, for God has brought good out of the evil you did to me. Because I was a slave in Egypt, I can now save my family from starvation."

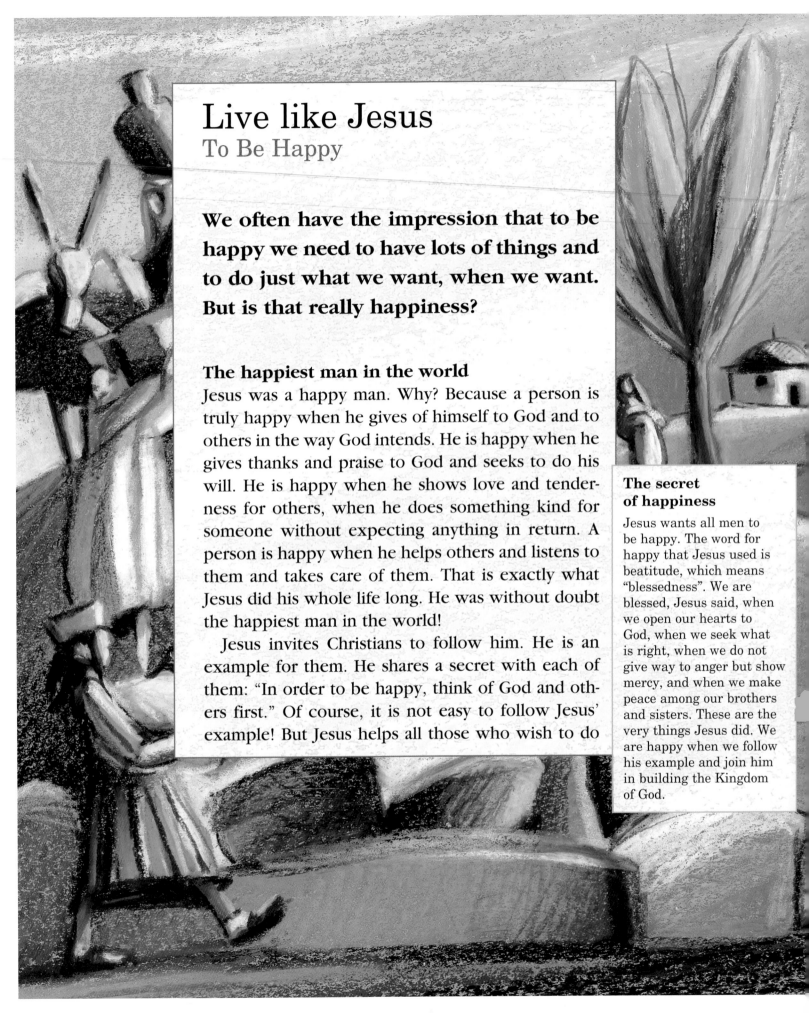

Live like Jesus
To Be Happy

We often have the impression that to be happy we need to have lots of things and to do just what we want, when we want. But is that really happiness?

The happiest man in the world

Jesus was a happy man. Why? Because a person is truly happy when he gives of himself to God and to others in the way God intends. He is happy when he gives thanks and praise to God and seeks to do his will. He is happy when he shows love and tenderness for others, when he does something kind for someone without expecting anything in return. A person is happy when he helps others and listens to them and takes care of them. That is exactly what Jesus did his whole life long. He was without doubt the happiest man in the world!

Jesus invites Christians to follow him. He is an example for them. He shares a secret with each of them: "In order to be happy, think of God and others first." Of course, it is not easy to follow Jesus' example! But Jesus helps all those who wish to do

The secret of happiness

Jesus wants all men to be happy. The word for happy that Jesus used is beatitude, which means "blessedness". We are blessed, Jesus said, when we open our hearts to God, when we seek what is right, when we do not give way to anger but show mercy, and when we make peace among our brothers and sisters. These are the very things Jesus did. We are happy when we follow his example and join him in building the Kingdom of God.

so. He does not leave them on their own. He sends them his Spirit to give them his strength.

Having all the things we want is not what brings happiness! Doing whatever we want is not what brings joy! It is loving God and others that makes us happy.

Turning our hearts toward God

Sometimes we realize that we are on the wrong track. When this happens, we can change course and turn our hearts toward God. The word for this change of heart is conversion. We do not convert ourselves once and for all. We must go on doing it over and over, choosing to follow God again and again. This is the road to happiness.

Mary
A Yes for a Lifetime

Mary was the Mother of Jesus. She carried him in her arms. She helped him grow up. She was there when he performed miracles. She knew his friends. And then she followed him right to the foot of the Cross. She showed all of us the way to follow Jesus.

A very simple life

Mary was a simple girl from a small town in Galilee. Yet it was she whom God chose to be the Mother of Jesus.

In an earlier chapter* is the story of how Jesus was born. Forty days after his birth, Mary went to the Temple with Joseph to present her Son to God. She understood that Jesus did not belong only to her; above all, he belonged to God.

At a wedding in Cana, Mary told Jesus that the wine had run out. She had total faith in her Son, knowing that he had come to bring joy to the world. Jesus listened to his Mother and performed a miracle: he turned water into wine!

When Jesus was nailed to the Cross, Mary was still by his side. She never abandoned him. She suffered but remained standing

*Pages 42-43.

> **Hail Mary**
>
> Hail Mary,
> full of grace.
> The Lord is with thee.
> Blessed art thou among women,
> and blessed is the fruit
> of thy womb, Jesus.
> Holy Mary,
> Mother of God,
> pray for us sinners,
> now and at the hour
> of our death.
> Amen.

there, ready to obey the will of God. From the Cross, Jesus told the apostle John, "Behold your mother." To Mary, he said, "Behold your son." So Mary is the mother of all who become the brothers and sisters of her Son.

Mary's good example

Mary did not speak much. She did not busy herself with lots of activities. She prayed and took care of her family. Those who believe in God admire her faith, her trust, the way she did exactly what Jesus expected of her, the way she said yes even when she did not fully understand what was going to happen. She was first and foremost the servant of the Lord. Mary is a wonderful example for us.

The Rosary

A rosary looks like a long necklace with many beads and a cross or crucifix. It has five sections with ten beads each, called decades. While holding each of these beads in turn, we pray a Hail Mary and remember an important event in the lives of Mary and Jesus.

147

The Saints
They Show the Way to God

The lives of the saints contain stories that astound us, thrill us, or inspire us. And yet, saints are not superheroes. God would like everyone to be a saint.

The saints have their faults!

Saint Jerome was irritable. Saint Paul often got angry. Saint Thomas Aquinas had a weakness for food. Saint Catherine of Siena quarreled even with the pope. The saints had their faults, but they loved God more than anything. As a result, they grew to be more and more like Jesus. Some of them performed miracles in his name, and some gave their lives for him.

Thousands of saints

There have been saints in all ages and all places. There are the saints in the Church calendar and

many others besides. There are countless ways to be a saint. There are saints who were priests or religious and others who were married. Some saints were children like you.

Follow!

We can pray to the saints we like most: our patron saint, our family's saint, a saint whose life we have read. Saints help us to discover God. They are like big brothers and sisters who show us the right road. They invite us Christians to set off on our way. But be careful: you must not try to do everything exactly the way they did! Each one of us must find our own way to walk with Jesus.

Modern saints

Here are saints from the twentieth century. Maybe you will be a saint of the twenty-first!

Saint José Sánchez del Río—child martyr of Mexico
Saints Jacinta and Francisco Marto—children who saw Our Lady of Fatima
Saint Pio of Pietrelcina—priest and miracle worker
Saint Teresa Benedicta of the Cross—Jewish convert, scholar, nun, and martyr
Saint Gianna Molla—wife, mother, and doctor
Servant of God Fr. Emil Kapaun—chaplain to American soldiers during the Korean War

Prayer
A True Encounter with God

It is not always easy to talk about prayer. It is very personal, because each person relates to God in a unique way.

A conversation with God

Praying is not simply saying formal prayers we know by heart. It means entering God's presence, opening our hearts to him, and thinking of nothing but him. It is a conversation with God, in which we speak to him and listen to him. Of course, it is not always easy to pray, because we cannot see God or touch him. We must enter into prayer little by little and not let distractions stop us.

How do I pray?

Pray with your whole body. You can sit down to listen and be attentive, or you can stand up to show you are ready to follow Jesus. You can also kneel to be humble before God. You can close your eyes to concentrate better or clap and sing to show your joy and to praise the Lord. You can sit before a statue or icon with a lit candle.

You can pray anywhere: in a church, in your room, outside, or at school. You can pray anytime: at night before you go to sleep, before lunch, when

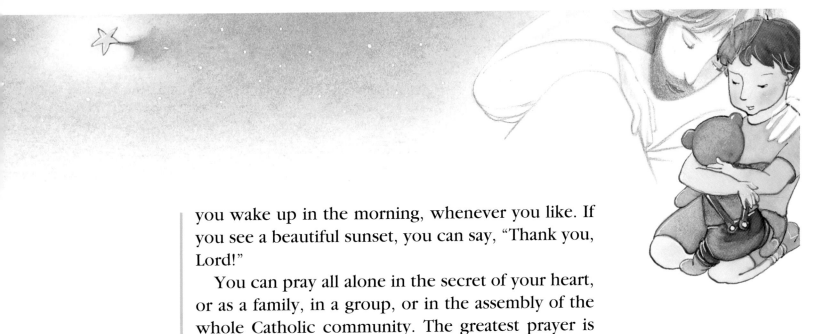

you wake up in the morning, whenever you like. If you see a beautiful sunset, you can say, "Thank you, Lord!"

You can pray all alone in the secret of your heart, or as a family, in a group, or in the assembly of the whole Catholic community. The greatest prayer is the Mass.

Will prayer change my life?

What is prayer for? Sometimes we pray for something that never happens. Then we might think there is no point in praying. That is not true: prayer that unites us to God is always good, but not always in the way we imagine. We pray first to allow God to transform us. When we pray, we open our hearts with trust. We ask God to change us for the better. Prayer is not magic, which seeks to control people or things. Prayer is giving everything and everyone to God.

When you pray, do not forget to say:

I love you
Thank you
I'm sorry
Please

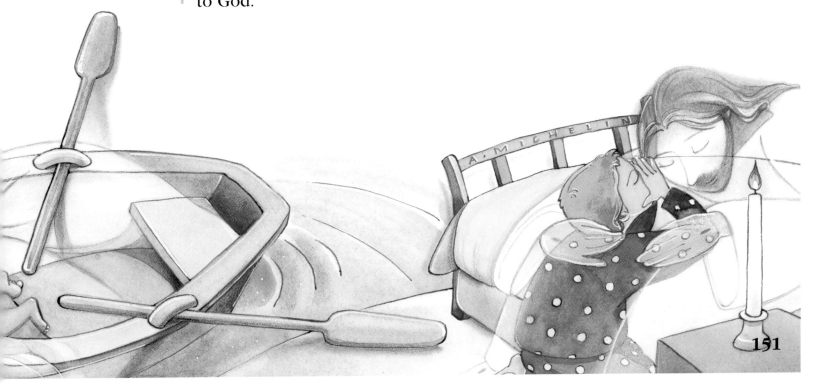

I Am Growing
Body and Soul

We were all babies once, not knowing how to walk or to talk. And then one day, thanks to good food and lots of love, we realize that we have grown. We have become a big boy or a big girl and dream of the day we will be a grown-up.

Growing up is a great adventure!
Turn the pages of a photo album, and you will see how the children in the photos have grown and how the adults' faces have changed. We never stop growing and changing. It is an exciting adventure but a little scary too, because the unknown frightens us a little!

As we grow up, we become aware that there is a time for everything. When you were a baby, your parents thought you were so cute when you sucked your thumb. Now that you are big, you know it looks pretty silly to suck your thumb, especially in front of other people!

You realize that your body is growing: your pants get too short, and your shoes get so small that they pinch your toes!

You know it takes a long time to grow from a baby to an adult. To become a grown-up means learning to be responsible for yourself and for others.

When you were a baby, you always needed others. As you grow up, you are able to help others in turn. Growing up is a great delight: you understand more and more complicated things and explore unknown subjects. You are constantly learning.

Do not be in a hurry!

Children are often in a hurry to grow up, but you must be patient. Look at a cathedral: it did not just pop out of the ground overnight. It took so many hours, days, and years of work! Look at nature: a seed takes many years to grow into a tree. You must not be in a hurry. You will grow little by little.

Do not forget to let your heart grow!

Growing up means letting your heart grow too. Your heart grows as you learn to love others more and more, to help them, to share with them, to put up with their faults. God is happy to see his children growing up, and he gives us his love to help us grow. He does not leave us on our own! He gives us strength to behave more and more wisely.

Growing

Did you know:
It is always at night while we sleep that our bodies grow. During the day, we are very busy growing our hearts and our minds. All through life, every month, our hair grows almost an inch, and our fingernails one-tenth of an inch.

153

Choices
You Can Say Yes or No

Your mom asks you to clean up your room. Do you stop playing and start cleaning, or do you pretend you did not hear her? When you do mischief, do you admit it, or do you hide it? The choice is up to you! So, are you free to do whatever you like?

It is up to you to decide!

At every moment of your life, you make choices: to keep quiet or to speak, to listen to your teacher or to daydream, to sulk or to join in with others, to help someone who is struggling or to let him down. It is not only big choices that shape our lives. Small daily choices mold us into the persons we become.

A difficult choice

When we are very young, we need others to make choices for us. Then one day, we are able to make decisions for ourselves. We become responsible for our actions.

It is not always easy to make choices. Things are not always black and white! Sometimes we are unsure because we want to say yes and no at the same time. But that is not possible! We must choose by deciding what is best. Sometimes one choice

is as good as another—such as whether to have vanilla or chocolate ice cream. The worst thing in this case would be not to make up your mind at all! Other times we must choose between good and bad—such as whether to tell our parents the truth about breaking something that belongs to them.

God created man free to choose the life he leads. This freedom is a wonderful gift, but using it correctly can sometimes be difficult and require courage. God does not leave us on our own. Jesus showed us how to choose. He also gave us the Golden Rule: treat others the way you want them to treat you.

Ask for help!

When you have trouble making a decision, first and foremost ask your parents to help you. A good teacher or your parish priest might be able to give you guidance too. Sometimes your friends can help, but they are as young as you are and do not have the wisdom of a grown-up. Never forget that God is there to help you. Ask him to guide you to the right choice!

Forgiving
Making Peace

Guns are laid down on the ground, people hug and shake hands, a child throws himself into his father's arms, a smile lights up a face: all of these are signs of peace. But making peace can be difficult.

Where is peace?
There is no peace when there is war between countries, arguments in a family, bullying on the playground, or hatred between neighbors. There is no peace where there is no justice, where there is theft, where people do not share. There is no peace when hearts are full of envy and anger, when mouths are full of bitter words.

Peace is up to all of us
Peace is the business of everyone, whether young or old. To make peace is to forgive your brother, your sister, your friends. It is also to ask for forgiveness. To make peace is to say good things instead of bad, to share instead of being greedy, to tell the truth instead of lying.

Jesus was a man of peace

Jesus asks Christians to be men of peace too. "Love your enemies," he said, "pray for those who do you harm!" And Jesus practiced what he preached: he prayed for his enemies who had him put to death on the Cross.

Pray for peace

Sometimes it makes us sad when someone does not want to make peace with us. It is like a heavy weight on our heart. In such a case, you must pray for peace and wait. Only God can move hearts.

And what about war?

In certain very serious cases, it is necessary to use force to stop people from doing something unjust. We call a policeman to stop a burglary, for example. Countries sometimes send soldiers to stop violence against their people or their friends. But even in such cases, we must respect our enemies and work and pray for peace.

Sharing
Building a Fairer World

Sharing sometimes requires effort. If you share a cake you do not like much, that is not so difficult! But to decide to give away your favorite toy, that is a lot more difficult! Do you understand why people must share?

Everything belongs to God

Sometimes people think the world belongs only to them and they can live however they like without any regard for anyone else. But God created the world for the benefit of everyone, and he entrusted its care to mankind. He asks men and women to act justly. What does that mean? That means respecting the rights of others and caring about their needs. If others are happy, we share their joy; if they are sick or mistreated, we share their suffering and help them.

For example, sharing might mean serving hot meals to the hungry or the homeless; it might mean visiting the sick in the hospital; it might mean put-

ting on a show for elderly people in a retirement home. Quite simply, sharing is being generous with what we have to make life better for others.

Even a child can share

To share means to give what we have. When you are little, you do not have much money, but you can still give something important. You can give your time, your attention, and your joyful presence. To give fifteen minutes out of your day to a grandparent or to the elderly lady next door—that is sharing. To invite home a schoolmate who has no friends—that is sharing. You can give so much joy to others simply by smiling and being polite. If everyone did that, the world would become a more beautiful place.

Group sharing

Many Christians have founded organizations to help those whose lives are difficult.
In almost every American parish, for example, there is a Saint Vincent de Paul Society that helps the poor. There are groups all around you: without making a fuss, thousands of people help others. In their quiet way, they are creating a better world right where you live.

A Time to Play
And a Time to Work

Matthew and Sophie are children just like you. They get up in the morning to go to school. They like to play with their friends, ride their bikes in the neighborhood, watch TV, and read stories at bedtime. During vacation, they go boating with their dad. What fun!

It is so nice to have fun!
It is important to play: it is a part of growing up. God is happy to see his children have fun. Sometimes Matthew plays on his own in his room. Sophie likes to make up stories. With their little sister, they perform shows for their parents. It is so much fun to get dressed up in costumes! And when they are invited to a birthday party, how great it is to laugh with their friends all afternoon!

Learning is important
Maybe you feel like playing all the time, but that is not possible! There is a time for everything. There is a time to play and a time to go to school. Learning to read, write, and do arithmetic is interesting. Discovering the history of mankind and the secrets of nature is fascinating. Of course, you learn in order

You are lucky to go to school!
There are still children in the world today who cannot go to school. They do menial, often difficult jobs just to earn enough to eat.

to become a responsible grown-up later on. But you also learn, quite simply, in order to love the world God created.

So many ways to learn!

You can learn from teachers at school or from books. You can also learn from people in your family. Listen to your parents; they know a lot! Ask your grandparents what it was like when they were little. They know even more than your parents do.

Matthew goes to catechism class

To increase his knowledge of God and his Church, along with other children his age Matthew goes to catechism class. At school, he learns math and science. In catechism class, he learns about the Bible and Jesus. He learns about the Mass and the other sacraments.

The Sacraments
Signs of God's Love

When we love someone, we like to give our love through words and actions. Husbands and wives kiss and speak kind words to each other. Parents give their children hugs and encouragement. Friends spend time together and help each other. God, too, gives his love and his life to us through signs. These are the sacraments.

Confession
God forgives those who are sorry for their sins. He gives them the strength to do the good they want to do and to avoid sin.

Baptism
God invites all men and women to be part of his family. He washes away their sins in the waters of baptism and gives them new life in Christ. This gift of God's life is called grace, and it makes us God's beloved children.

Communion
When we receive Communion, we receive the very life of Jesus in order to be one with him and become like him.

162

Holy orders

This is the sacrament God gives to bishops, priests, and deacons so they can give the sacraments to his people through the power of Christ.

Confirmation

God gives us the power of his Holy Spirit, so that we can make his love known to everyone on earth.

The Holy Spirit

Jesus came into the world to reconcile all men with God. Through signs, he gave men forgiveness, healing, and new life. Today, we no longer see Jesus, but through the Holy Spirit, he gives us grace, which is the life of God, through the sacraments of the Church.

Marriage

God blesses husbands and wives so that they may love each other all their lives and welcome children into the world. Their love for each other is an image of God's love for us.

Anointing of the sick

God gives his strength to those who are sick so that they may recover their health or have the patience and courage to endure their suffering.

Baptism
Becoming a Child of God

My name is Mathilda. Today is the baptism of my baby brother Dominic. Mom and Dad are Catholics, and they want Dominic to be a part of the great family of the friends of Jesus in the Catholic Church.

The preparations

Before we leave to go to the church, Mom dresses Dominic in a long white gown. Dad explained that white is the color for purity. Today, Dominic will be given the spotless life of Jesus.

The whole family is there in front of the church: Grandma, my aunts and uncles, and all our cousins. Mom and Dad asked Uncle Tony and Aunt Cathy to be Dominic's godfather and godmother. Mom and Dad trust them to love Dominic always and to help him know Jesus.

Inside the church, the priest welcomes Dominic. He makes the Sign of the Cross on his forehead. The Sign of the Cross is made by Catholics whenever they pray.

My cousin William reads a text from the Bible. Then Mom and Dad state that they wish to have Dominic baptized.

Those who are not baptized

God desires that everyone be baptized. Sadly, not everyone hears about Jesus or understands his invitation to become part of his Church. Those who are baptized are called upon to proclaim the good news of God's love and to pray that all men say yes to God's grace.

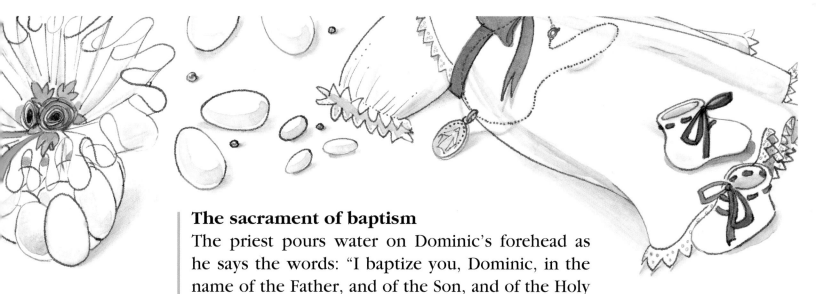

The sacrament of baptism

The priest pours water on Dominic's forehead as he says the words: "I baptize you, Dominic, in the name of the Father, and of the Son, and of the Holy Spirit." The water poured on his forehead is like a bath, which washes away the old life of sin and replaces it with the new life of Jesus. This life can undergo death and still last forever.

The priest marks Dominic's forehead with a perfumed oil. This is the sign that the Holy Spirit has come upon him to give him the strength to remain faithful to Jesus throughout his whole life.

Then we light a candle that symbolizes the light of Christ. From now on, that light will burn in Dominic's heart and shine out to others. After we leave the church, the celebration continues at our house. All my relatives come over for a special meal, and many of them bring gifts for baby Dominic.

Can you be baptized at any age?

When a baby is baptized, it is the parents' decision. When an older child or an adult is baptized, he himself makes the decision to be baptized. Usually people who are baptized when they are older receive the sacrament of confirmation at the same time. Catholics who were baptized as infants usually are confirmed when they are old enough to understand what it means to follow Jesus. Through confirmation, a Catholic receives the strength and the gifts of the Holy Spirit that he needs to live as a mature Christian and to make Jesus known to those around him.

Communion
Receiving the Life of Jesus

Jason and Tessa will soon make their First Holy Communion. Along with their friends in catechism class, they have learned that Communion is the most beautiful of gifts: the very life of Jesus.

The Last Supper

On the evening before he died, Jesus shared a last meal with his apostles. It was the Passover, when Jews celebrate their freedom from slavery in Egypt. Jesus wanted his friends to understand that his death and Resurrection would be the Passover for the whole world.

Through words and gestures, Jesus explained the meaning of his death. He took bread and blessed it. He broke the bread into pieces, saying, "Take this, all of you, and eat of it, for this is my Body, which will be given up for you." He took a cup of wine and said, "Take this, all of you, and drink from it, for this is the chalice of my Blood, the Blood of the new and eternal covenant, which will be poured out for you and for many for the forgiveness of sins. Do this in memory of me." Ever since, this is what the priest does and what Catholics participate in at each Mass. It is called the celebration of the Eucharist.

Is Jesus really there?

The command *"Do this in remembrance of me"* does not mean just to recall what Jesus said and did two thousand years ago. It means to make present again the action of Jesus when he gave his life. We do not see Jesus with our eyes, but through the words and gestures of the priest, who acts in the person of Christ, the bread and wine are transformed into the same gift that Jesus gave to his apostles. When we receive Communion, we see a morsel of bread, but we believe that in this way Jesus gives us his own life.

God wishes people to live in him

We need food to live. The food we usually eat is digested and becomes part of us. When we receive the Body and Blood of Christ, something else happens: we become part of Jesus. When we are baptized, we become part of Jesus too, but we can be baptized only once. To sustain our life in Jesus, we need to stay as close to him as possible, and the best way to do this is by receiving Communion as often as we can.

A rendezvous with God

The big day has arrived, and Jason and Tessa are deeply moved. Their parents are so happy: their children are really growing up in the faith! This will be the First Communion for Jason and Tessa, but it will not end there: from now on they will have a rendezvous with Jesus each Sunday at Mass. Little by little, they will come to know Jesus better and better.

Confession

Before they received their First Holy Communion, Jason and Tessa confessed their sins to a priest for the first time. Since they are young, they did not have terrible things to confess, but beforehand they asked the Holy Spirit to help them to recall the ways they had freely chosen to hurt others or to disobey their parents. When we confess even small sins to a priest, we receive not only forgiveness but the grace to do better.

167

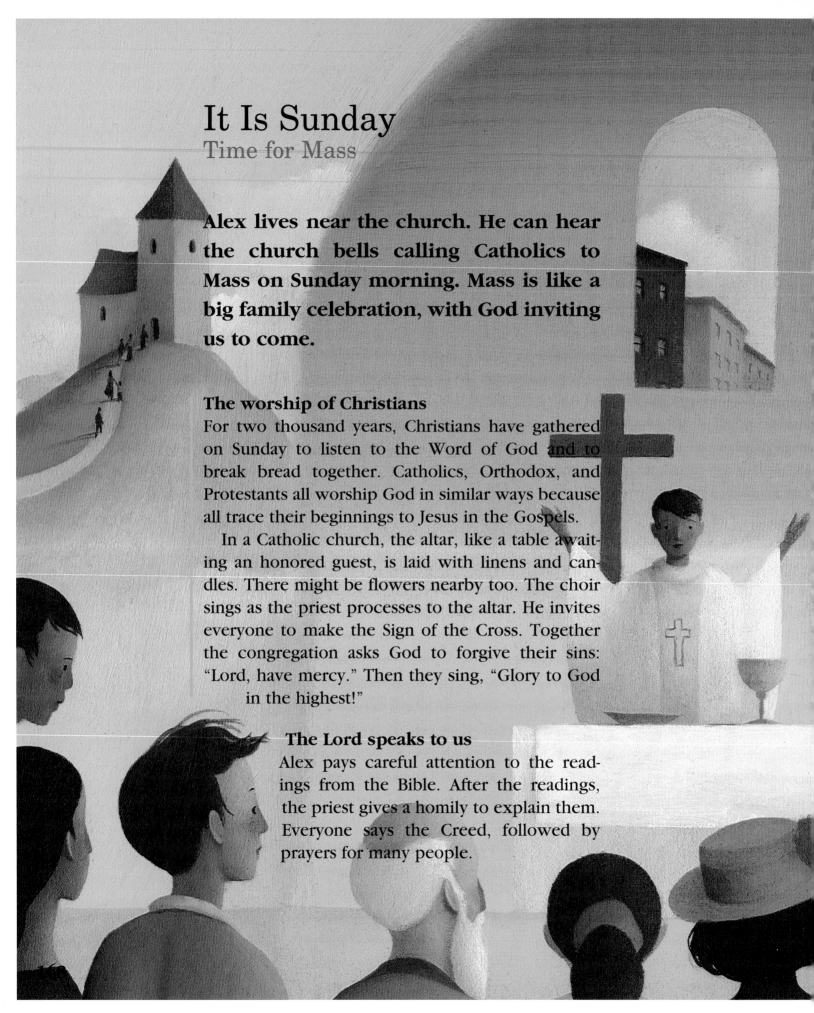

It Is Sunday
Time for Mass

Alex lives near the church. He can hear the church bells calling Catholics to Mass on Sunday morning. Mass is like a big family celebration, with God inviting us to come.

The worship of Christians

For two thousand years, Christians have gathered on Sunday to listen to the Word of God and to break bread together. Catholics, Orthodox, and Protestants all worship God in similar ways because all trace their beginnings to Jesus in the Gospels.

In a Catholic church, the altar, like a table awaiting an honored guest, is laid with linens and candles. There might be flowers nearby too. The choir sings as the priest processes to the altar. He invites everyone to make the Sign of the Cross. Together the congregation asks God to forgive their sins: "Lord, have mercy." Then they sing, "Glory to God in the highest!"

The Lord speaks to us

Alex pays careful attention to the readings from the Bible. After the readings, the priest gives a homily to explain them. Everyone says the Creed, followed by prayers for many people.

The Lord feeds us

A family brings the bread and wine to the priest. He says a prayer of thanksgiving to God. The congregation sings, "Holy, holy, holy . . ." and kneels. The priest asks God to send his Holy Spirit over the bread and wine, so that they may become the Body and Blood of Jesus. He says the words of the Consecration: "Take this, all of you . . . " He prays for all people, living or dead. Along with everyone else, Alex stands and says the prayer that Jesus taught us: the Our Father. Then the people give each other the peace of Christ. Next they sing, "Lamb of God, you take away the sins of the world . . .", and they kneel again.

Then the priest invites the people to receive the Body of Christ. "Lord, I am not worthy . . ." Alex goes forward and receives Communion. "Thank you, Jesus", he says, conversing God in the silence of his heart.

The Lord sends out his messengers

The priest blesses the people and sends them forth to share the love of Jesus with others. "Thanks be to God", everyone says.

169

Vocation
A Calling from God

Ever since Carlos and Amelia visited the monastery, they have been asking a lot of questions. Why do some men and women decide to devote their lives to prayer? Why do some men become priests? Why did their mom and dad decide to get married and have a family? And what will they do when they grow up?

God calls everyone

God calls every person to the way of life that will make him happy. Some he calls to be priests, monks, or nuns. Most he calls to married life. This calling from God is a vocation. To find your vocation, you should pray. God is the best guide, because he knows you, and loves you, and wishes for your happiness more than anyone else does. God speaks to you through the deepest desires of your heart and through the example and wise counsel of others.

How do you become a priest?

When a boy thinks that God is calling him to be a priest, he speaks to a priest about it. Sometime during or after college, he enters a seminary, where other young men like him pray and study the Word of God and the teachings of the Church. When the bishop thinks that he is ready, he ordains him a deacon and then, about a year later, a priest. To be ordained by the bishop is to be called to administer the sacraments with him in the name of Christ and his Church. There are also religious orders of priests, such as the Jesuits and the Dominicans. These have their own programs for the training of priests.

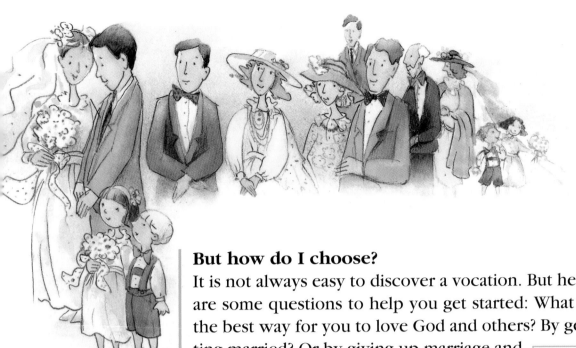

But how do I choose?

It is not always easy to discover a vocation. But here are some questions to help you get started: What is the best way for you to love God and others? By getting married? Or by giving up marriage and a family of your own in order to serve the family of God as a priest, sister, or brother? The best choice is the one that is best for your salvation. When you experience great peace and joy in your heart, you will know you are on the right track.

Christian marriage

Marriage is a beautiful vocation. For their children, their friends, and all those they encounter, a husband and wife are a living image of the love of God.

171

Marriage
A Man and a Woman Become One

My name is Clarissa. Today is a celebration! My cousin Christopher is getting married to Nicole. They are both smiling as if this were the most wonderful day in their lives. Their families are happy to be gathered around them.

To love each other for the rest of their lives

One day Christopher met Nicole. He noticed her right away! At first, they hardly knew each other. But, little by little, they discovered that they truly loved each other. They decided to get married. Marriage is a big step: it is a promise between a man and a woman to love each other faithfully for the rest of their lives. That is only natural! When you love someone, you never want it to end and never want to be separated.

Christopher and Nicole are Catholics. They believe that God is the source of their love. They want to become one in Christ so that Jesus will always be by their side to give them the strength to go on loving each other even when times are hard.

> **Marriage is a sacrament**
>
> It is a sign: a bride and groom stand together before the altar, giving their lives to God and to each other. It is a promise: they exchange vows before God. It gives grace: through their love for each other, God gives them his life. He helps them to be generous to each other and to welcome children as gifts from him.

The great day of the marriage

In a very beautiful celebration in the church, Christopher and Nicole promise, with the help of God, to love each other for the rest of their lives. There are lots of flowers. Their friends have organized the music. Children sit in the front row to get the best view of everything that is happening. The couple is filled with emotion. This is what they say to each other, before God, the priest, their witnesses, and everyone gathered in the church:

"I, Christopher, take you, Nicole, to be my wife. I promise to be true to you in good times and in bad, in sickness and in health. I will love you and honor you all the days of my life."

"I, Nicole, take you, Christopher, to be my husband . . ."

Christopher and Nicole exchange rings, saying, "I give you this ring as a sign of my love and fidelity."

They promise to teach their future children about Jesus.

After the ceremony, everyone gets together to continue the celebration. There is cake and champagne. There is joy and dancing until late in the night. Everyone is happy!

Divorce

Divorce is always sad. It is wounding for the husband, the wife, and the children. It is the death of love. Divorced Catholics still remain Catholic. God is unchanging: he does not withdraw the love he gave them at their baptism. The Church asks divorced Catholics not to remarry, because they promised to love each other for the rest of their lives and became one.

173

Through the Year with Jesus
The Liturgical Calendar

After autumn comes winter, with its cold and, in some places, snow. In the spring, the fields are covered with flowers. In summer, children go swimming at the beach. It is a little like that in the life of a Christian. Throughout the year, Christians relive the great events in the life of Jesus. The Catholic Church keeps track of these events with her liturgical calendar.

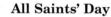

All Saints' Day
On November 1, we honor the saints of all times and places, known and unknown, who did the will of the Lord. On November 2, All Souls' Day, we pray for all the dead, that they may join the company of saints in heaven.

The Assumption
On August 15, we commemorate the Assumption of Mary, who was taken, body and soul, to heaven. She is a sign of hope for all Christians.

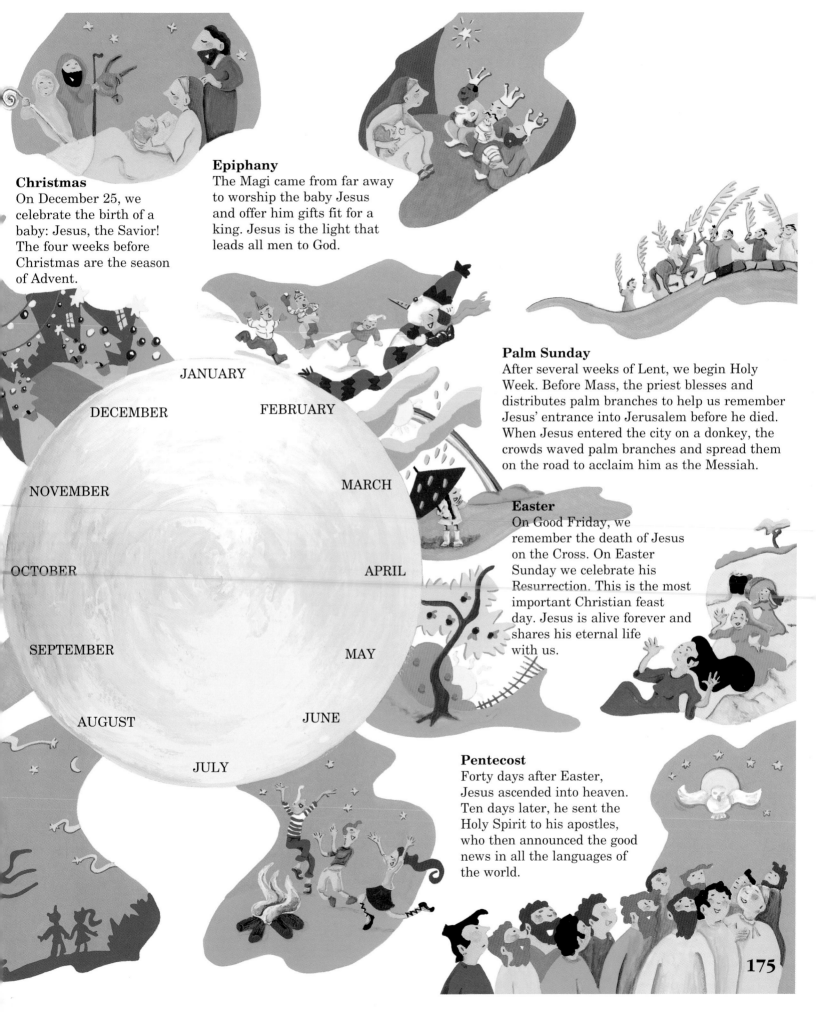

Christmas
On December 25, we celebrate the birth of a baby: Jesus, the Savior! The four weeks before Christmas are the season of Advent.

Epiphany
The Magi came from far away to worship the baby Jesus and offer him gifts fit for a king. Jesus is the light that leads all men to God.

Palm Sunday
After several weeks of Lent, we begin Holy Week. Before Mass, the priest blesses and distributes palm branches to help us remember Jesus' entrance into Jerusalem before he died. When Jesus entered the city on a donkey, the crowds waved palm branches and spread them on the road to acclaim him as the Messiah.

Easter
On Good Friday, we remember the death of Jesus on the Cross. On Easter Sunday we celebrate his Resurrection. This is the most important Christian feast day. Jesus is alive forever and shares his eternal life with us.

Pentecost
Forty days after Easter, Jesus ascended into heaven. Ten days later, he sent the Holy Spirit to his apostles, who then announced the good news in all the languages of the world.

JANUARY

DECEMBER

FEBRUARY

NOVEMBER

MARCH

OCTOBER

APRIL

SEPTEMBER

MAY

AUGUST

JUNE

JULY

Illustrators

■ Pierre and Elisabeth Baulig
18, 20, 44, 46, 58, 60, 98, 148, 166, 170.

■ Andrée Bienfait
22, 40, 48, 90, 94, 104, 124.

■ Florence Delclos
120, 140, 142, 152, 154, 156, 158, 160, 174.

■ Bruno Le Sourd
32, 50, 74, 84, 102, 106, 112.

■ Frédérick Mansot
14, 24, 30, 34, 56, 76, 88, 100.

■ Anne Michelin
10, 38, 42, 52, 62, 68, 86,122, 128, 134, 136,
146, 150, 164, 172.

■ Sylvie Montmoulineix
12, 26, 54, 130, 132, 138, 144.

■ Eric Puybaret
16, 36, 64, 72, 80, 116, 162, 168.

■ Christophe Verdenal
28, 66, 74, 78, 82, 92, 96, 108, 110, 114, 126.

■ Carine Sanson
Cover

Original French edition: *Theo Benjamin, L'Encyclopédie catholique pour les enfants*

© 2009 by Groupe Fleurus, Paris.
© 2013 by Magnificat, New York - Ignatius Press, San Francisco.
All rights reserved
ISBN Ignatius Press 978-1-58617-813-0. ISBN MAGNIFICAT 978-1-936260-55-3
The trademark MAGNIFICAT depicted in this publication is used under license from and
is the exclusive property of Magnificat Central Service Team, Inc., A ministry to Catholic Women,
and may not be used without its written consent.

Printed by Tien Wah Press, Singapore
Printed on August 2014
Job number MGN 14014-R1
Printed in France in compliance with the Consumer Protection Safety Act, 2008.